Education, Individualization and Neoliberalism

Bloomsbury Critical Education series

Series editor: Peter Mayo

This series is fundamentally concerned with the relationship between education and power in society and is therefore committed to publishing volumes containing insights into ways of confronting inequalities and social exclusions in different learning settings and society at large. The series will comprise books wherein authors contend forthrightly with the inextricability of power/knowledge relations.

Also available from Bloomsbury

Pedagogy, Politics and Philosophy of Peace,
edited by Carmel Borg and Michael Grech

Critical Human Rights, Citizenship, and Democracy Education,
edited by Michalinos Zembylas and André Keet

Course Syllabi in Faculties of Education,
edited by André Elias Mazawi and Michelle Stack

Education, Individualization and Neoliberalism,
by Valerie Visanich

Education, Individualization and Neoliberalism

Youth in Southern Europe

Valerie Visanich

BLOOMSBURY ACADEMIC
LONDON • NEW YORK • OXFORD • NEW DELHI • SYDNEY

BLOOMSBURY ACADEMIC
Bloomsbury Publishing Plc
50 Bedford Square, London, WC1B 3DP, UK
1385 Broadway, New York, NY 10018, USA
29 Earlsfort Terrace, Dublin 2, Ireland

BLOOMSBURY, BLOOMSBURY ACADEMIC and the Diana logo
are trademarks of Bloomsbury Publishing Plc

First published in Great Britain 2020
This paperback edition published 2023

Copyright © Valerie Visanich
Valerie Visanich has asserted her right under the Copyright, Designs
and Patents Act, 1988, to be identified as Author of this work.

For legal purposes the Acknowledgements on p. xiv constitute
an extension of this copyright page.

Series design by Catherine Wood
Cover image © Studiojumpee/Shutterstock

All rights reserved. No part of this publication may be reproduced or transmitted
in any form or by any means, electronic or mechanical, including photocopying,
recording, or any information storage or retrieval system, without prior permission
in writing from the publishers.

Bloomsbury Publishing Plc does not have any control over, or responsibility for,
any third-party websites referred to or in this book. All internet addresses given
in this book were correct at the time of going to press. The author and publisher
regret any inconvenience caused if addresses have changed or sites have
ceased to exist, but can accept no responsibility for any such changes.

A catalogue record for this book is available from the British Library.

Library of Congress Cataloging-in-Publication Data

Names: Visanich, Valerie, author.
Title: Education, individualization and neoliberalism: youth in Southern Europe / Valerie Visanich.
Description: London; New York: Bloomsbury Academic, 2020. |
Series: Bloomsbury critical education | Includes bibliographical references and index. |
Summary: "Education, Individualization and Neoliberalism questions the individualization process
in education in the Anglo-American context and analyses how this process is applied in the
everyday life of millennials with tertiary education in Southern Europe. Valerie Visanich explores the close
affinity of this concept to neoliberalism in contemporary societies, specifically by focusing on
changes in education and employment. Using Beck & Beck-Gernsheim's concept of individualization to refer to
increased freedom in one's life choices yet at the same time increased risks, Visanich unpacks the
trajectories of life experiences of tertiary educated millennials in the contemporary neoliberal Anglo-American setting
in relation to recent cultural and socio-economic changes. She examines how this
individualized mode is adopted and adapted in countries across Southern Europe including Italy, Spain, Portugal,
Malta and Greece - in locations where cultural conditions habitually cushion-out, often by family
networks and patronage, some of the burdens of being young today"– Provided by publisher.
Identifiers: LCCN 2020009116 (print) | LCCN 2020009117 (ebook) |
ISBN 9781350082458 (hardback) | ISBN 9781350082465 (ebook) | ISBN 9781350082472 (epub)
Subjects: LCSH: Education, Higher–Economic aspects–Europe, Southern–Cross-cultural studies. |
Generation Y–Europe, Southern–Economic conditions–Cross-cultural studies. |
Generation Y–Education (Higher)–Europe, Southern–Cross-cultural studies. |
Neoliberalism–Europe, Southern–Cross-cultural studies. | Individuality–Europe, Southern–Cross-cultural studies.
Classification: LCC LC67.E854 V57 2020 (print) | LCC LC67.E854 (ebook) | DDC 378.4–dc23
LC record available at https://lccn.loc.gov/2020009116
LC ebook record available at https://lccn.loc.gov/2020009117

ISBN: HB: 978-1-3500-8245-8
PB: 978-1-3501-9248-5
ePDF: 978-1-3500-8246-5
ePUB: 978-1-3500-8247-2

Series: Bloomsbury Critical Education

Typeset by Integra Software Services Pvt. Ltd.

To find out more about our authors and books visit www.bloomsbury.com
and sign up for our newsletters.

In Memory of my mother Maria Dolores Visanich
(1948–2011)

What is it like to be a well-educated millennial in southern Europe?

Valerie Visanich *is a Senior Lecturer in Sociology at the University of Malta, Malta.*

Contents

Preface — xii
Acknowledgements — xiv

Introduction — 1
   On individualization and neoliberalism — 3
   Central questions of the book — 7
   Organization of content — 8
   On southern Europe — 10
   On youth — 13

1 The extension and expansion of education — 19
   Conceptualizing youth — 20
   Changes in the educational system in the last sixty years — 24
   How did this all change? — 27
   Changes in the educational system in southern Europe — 28
   Education and social mobility — 30

2 The currency of academic credentials, consumerism and financial burdens — 35
   Academic capitalism — 36
   The debt generation — 38
   The origins of consumer seduction for youth — 41
   Conspicuous consumption, marketing seduction and subcultural identities — 43
   The use of commodities: agency and subcultural capital — 46
   Cashing on counter-culture identities — 50
   Conclusion — 54

3 Unemployment in the graduate economy — 57
   The common post-war Anglo-American experience — 58

	Changes in the labour market	61
	The situation in the south	66
	Conclusion	68
4	Neoliberal intersubjectivity: A way of doing things	71
	The structure of feeling of millennials	72
	Changes from collective to individual: From welfare ideology to neoliberal subjectivity	78
	Personal branding and the culture of perfectionism	80
	Conclusion	84
5	Shock-Absorbers for youth in the South	85
	Welfare provisions in the South	87
	Family formation and kinship ties	89
	Leaving parental home	93
	Family responsibility and gendered roles	94
	Conclusion	99
6	Slow motion changes in the South: The case of a small Southern European state	101
	The Maltese case	102
	Malta's colonial and postcolonial status	104
	Historical overview on opportunities for higher education	107
	Economic shifts in recent years	110
	Application of laissez-faire measures and individualization	112
	The spread of neoliberalism and individualization: Inhibiting cultural agents	114
	Conclusion	117
7	The meanings and feelings of tertiary-educated millennials in the South	119
	Fieldwork	120
	Social types of individual life biographies	122
	Degree of agency	123
	The degree of anxiety	126

Negotiation and accommodation of cultural conditions 129
Education and the job market 132
Choices in consumption 134
Compromised choices in the lives of women 139
Conclusion 141

Summary and conclusions 143
   Recommendations 148
   End remarks 150

References 151
Index 169

Preface

The old adage that the more you study an issue the less clear it becomes fits perfectly the chosen topic of this book. Through acquiring a sociological imagination into the everyday life experiences of millennials in education and work, it becomes clear that the more you unpack and make sense of their situations, the more you outline incongruities in their present life situations and future aspirations. The generation of millennials, especially those with tertiary education, typify the paradox of living in the now. Their life experiences are arguably not as straightforward as previous generations of young adults. From a critical lens, they are considered as living within a socio-economic climate which is far from presenting them with prosperous conditions. They face increased demands from the educational system; they are enduring living with student loans well in their adulthood and are more prone to experience anxiety within an entrepreneurial culture that emphasizes self-branding, hard work and perfectionism. Being trained within a climate of rapid changes in the economy due to the intensification of neoliberalism, the encroachment of the market is etched in their everyday social and economic life. It is indeed the case, as maintained by Laurie Penny (2010:137), that

> the political psychology of this generation is unique. Our youth and adolescence passed in a bubble of neoliberal ideology that popped as we entered the job market, leaving us bereft .... We had imagined adult life as a broad and brutal trajectory, in which we would be thrust all alone onto the conveyor belt of neoliberal growth, obliged to scramble to stay in forward motion ... an inculcated fear of failure, we had accepted ceaseless toil and pocket-money wages. (Penny, 2010:137)

Yet they are also a generation which are technologically proficient, have more opportunities for post-compulsory education and are reflexively deciding what they want to do with their lives. Most of them also enjoy the benefits of advancement in health care and presumably will live longer than their predecessors. This constant oscillation between advantageous and unfavourable conditions is what makes this generation fascinating to study sociologically. It is not the scope here to give the impression that this is the first youth generation with its fair share of ambiguities and shifting tendencies – youth itself, as an intermediary stage in the life cycle, is a time period of opacity and transit – as addressed principally when exploring the transitory youth generation of baby boomers in the 1960s.

Specifically, this book unpacks the everyday life experiences of well-educated youth, within the Anglo-American context. It explores the applicability of this lifestyles in southern Europe – in locations where cultural conditions habitually cushion out, sometimes both by family networks and financial means, some of the burdens of being a young adult.

There are various issues that remain un(der)explored here. In view of this, I see this book as an evolving project on the bumpy ride of millennials living with new demands in the educational system, the job and consumer market in a neoliberal economic climate. With these prefatory remarks, this book proceeds to an exploration into the lives of these youth in question.

Acknowledgements

Working on a comprehensive study on the everyday life of millennials, living in the Anglo-American and the southern European context, proved to be an arduous task, albeit an exciting one. This rutted journey that started during my PhD studies in 2006 could not have been possible without the contribution of a number of academics, close friends and of course family members.

Firstly, I would like to thank the contributors to this series, in particular the editor Professor Peter Mayo for his extraordinary input and commitment to critical scholarship and practice in education.

There are also numerous friends whose scholarship, activism and advice I have benefitted from including Professor Jim McGuigan and Professor Chris Rojek, as well as my colleagues at the Department of Sociology within the University of Malta, whose advice sharpened my thoughts.

I would like to thank my husband Jonathan, for his forbearance, his continuous contribution and support to make this book possible. I would also like to thank my children Alexander and Victoria, for giving me the possibility to understand the structure of feeling of a different generation and for making me reflect better on how taken-for-granted dispositions are indeed substantially influenced by the culture of a particular period in time. Finally, many thanks go to my parents. Even though my mother did not live long enough to see the end of this work, her words of encouragement have driven me along the years to work harder in what sometimes seemed like an interminable task.

Introduction

'Stop buying avocado toast if you want to buy a home!' exclaimed Tim Gurner (Levin, 2017), a millionaire Australian property tycoon while dissing millennials for their spending habits. What today became an in-joke for millennials, a generational label given to those born roughly between the 1980s and mid-1990s, avocado toast is now a symbol of the young highly educated generation who spend money on frivolous things such as avocado and expensive coffee but cannot afford to leave their parental home. For some of these youth, their penchant for markers of privilege, including in their cultural currency to distinguish themselves, often typifies them as a generation who is very much class and cultural conscious, although it is too naïve to simply regard millennials as a slothful bunch, with highbrow predilections or as having idiosyncratic traits. This would simply suggest a kind of moral panic of a degenerative youth – a proposition that is far from a new phenomenon to describe youth.

Millennials share a culturally binding mode of attribution as being more reflexive than any other generation and having a firm stand in designing their life in an individualized manner. They lend themselves perfectly to maxims like 'live life to the full' yet 'your life, your failures'. This is particularly true for those with tertiary education, who were born with more opportunities to choose what they want to do with their lives. In upbeat moments, they would like to think of themselves as fully in control of what to do in their lives. Yet despite this fantastical dimension of the process of individualization, in reality they are also often too uncertain about their decisions, too anxious and the most egregiously of it all is they blame themselves for any failure such as unemployment. This is an issue that demands serious attention, especially within the context of an effervescent economic climate.

It is safe to say that millennials in Western societies were born neoliberals. Born during the application of neoliberalism in the Anglo-American context in the 1980s and 1990s, they were trained to internalize its creed as a personal mode of working. During their coming of age, neoliberalism became more strident. Neoliberalism has traditionally been understood in terms of its political and economic school of thought for its agenda to promote privatization, deregulation and limiting state support. Yet it had extended beyond socio-economic policies into an entrepreneurial mode of personal life.

In view of the rapid changes in the economy, this book advances a relational understanding of what is it like for the now thirty-something graduates, with middle-class aspirations, to juggle individualized lifestyles in a neoliberal climate. This book is not solely on the educational system, its expansion and extension, but it also explores the lives of millennials beyond tertiary education, in the labour market and their everyday life experiences in general. Specifically, it makes sense of highly educated youth and their personal claim on neoliberalism in their individualized life experiences as well as the complex emanation of the social interactions that produces them. In doing so, this book looks into the trajectories of lived experiences of these youth by examining the common Anglo-American processes of cultural, historical and socio-economic changes. It presents an understanding of the complex interrelations for youth today, living in what is often referred to, at times hyperbolically, as the age of anxiety.

Although this book is concerned with 'anxiety in ambivalence' – anxiety in ambivalent, peripheral locations in Europe – it questions the degree of individualization for highly educated youth, living at the fringes of southern European countries. Of course, this application is not linear; different policy adjustments and welfare regimes were applied across various southern European nations. In this regard, it is appropriate to examine the universal and local together, with the assumption that specificity of insights presents credibility to general knowledge. There are various prevalent common historical and cultural legacies of countries in the south, not only in their geographical proximity but also in their cultural commonalities; these include the role of familialism in the provision of welfare and the influence of religion in various areas of life.

The sociological relevance of this book is threefold. First, it underlines the need to interrogate how opportunities for tertiary education shape connections, relationships and life trajectories of millennials. Second, it demonstrates how economic and cultural conditions as well as social networks in peripheral locations in the South have a significant impact on the experiences of youth in education and employment. Third, it contributes to the literature on youth by presenting life experiences of millennials.

Hence, this book digs deep into examining the application of a neoliberal mentality in the southern context, as a co-construct and in mutual mediation with individualization. In a critical evaluation of the neoliberal system in education and work, this book acquires the 'sociological imagination' into the lives of individualized youth as a generation born, raised and fully immersed into a neoliberal economic climate. Here, I borrow C. Wright Mills's (1959) definition on the ability to be able to understand youths' personal challenges intertwined with social relations and larger political and economic context. In his own words:

> For that imagination is the capacity to shift from one perspective to another – from the political to the psychological; from examination of a single family to comparative assessment of the nation budgets of the world. ... It is the capacity to range from the most impersonal and remote transformations to the most intimate features of the human self – and to see the relations between the two. Back of its use there is always the urge to know the social and historical meaning of the individual in the society and in the period in which he has his quality and his being. (Mills, 1959:7)

On individualization and neoliberalism

> Individualisation is a social condition ... a compulsion, albeit a paradoxical one, to create, to stage manage, not only one's own biography but the bonds and networks surrounding it and to do this amid changing preferences and at successive stages of life, while constantly adapting to the conditions of the labour market, the educational system, the welfare state and so on. (Beck and Beck-Gernsheim, 2002[2008]:4)

There is hardly any other pervasive aspiration today than to devise your life on your own free-will. Beck and Beck-Gernsheim (2002) were master diagnosticians of our ills today. Even now, eighteen years after the publication of *Individualization*, their observation of life in late modernity remains entirely valid. In recent years, the new concept of agency arises alongside ideas on reflexivity, competition, autonomy and social organization. The concept of individualization is defined as a structural, sociological transformation of social institutions and the relationship of the individual and society … it has undermined traditional securities such as religious faith, and simultaneously it has created new forms of social commitments [The concept of individualization is used to] explore not just how people deal with these transformations in terms of their identity and consciousness, but also how their life situations and biographical patterns are changed (Beck and Beck-Gernsheim, 2008[2002]:202).

The concept of individualization is about this increased emphasis on individuality and self-reliance. While this concept may be perceived as producing a sense of subjective individuality, it must not be confused with individualism or individuation, as Beck and Beck-Gernsheim put it, 'a term used by depth psychologists to describe the process of becoming an autonomous individual' (2002[2008]:202).

> Individualization liberates people from traditional roles and constraints in a number of ways. First, individuals are removed from status-based classes. … Second, women are cut loose from their 'status fate' of compulsory housework and support by a husband. … Thirdly, the old forms of work routine and discipline are in decline with the emergence of flexible work hours, pluralized underemployment and the decentralization of work sites. (Beck and Beck-Gernsheim 2008[2002]:202–203)

Individualization is a dialectical process of disintegration and reinvention. People have become compelled to decide, plan and negotiate their own life-course transitions instead of following a traditional chronological order. The sequence of life passages is selected and organized by the individuals themselves. Individuals find their own solutions for the disruptions in society rather than relying on collective support systems and traditional structures. Individuals navigate their passage by developing a sense of self, rooted in a form of adult role that they decide to adopt (Côté, 2010). It is worth noting that the process of individualization is not referred to here in a deterministic sense but in terms of a revitalized discussion on the fluctuations in youth identities.

Herein, the concept of individualization is positioned in terms of the 'institutionalized individualism', very similar to what Beck and Beck-Gernsheim (2008[2002]) argued. Yet unlike the Becks who deny the connection between neoliberalism and individualization and stressed their distinguishable features, this book draws on the close similitude of both; how they co-exist within the same climate of self-reliance and disembeddedness. Whereas individualization has to do with the notion of increased personal choice, neoliberalism is an ideology of self-sufficiency.

The crisis of Keynesian organized capitalism coincided with the OPEC oil price hike of 1973 – a predicament that fuelled a right turn to a neoliberal economy. Economic growth driven by 'embedded liberalism' became exhausted and was 'no longer working' (Harvey, 2005:12). The only solution deemed viable was neoliberalism for individual choice and freedom – freedom from the bureaucratic system of central planning – a kind of freedom which may sound beguiling in general terms but its implications are arguably seen as a far cry from freedom. Having Chile as a 'pilot study' following General Pinochet's coup, neoliberalism has ever since become the main proponent of a global economic system through hegemonic means (Harvey, 2005). The conventional conceptualization of the neoliberal discourse is based on its effectiveness and efficiency. Discourse on the acceptance of the economic rationale of calculability as part of the everyday life is simply a reflection of its hegemonic stamp (Gorz, 1989).

Neoliberal politics encourage individuals 'to devise individual solutions to socially generated problems and to do it individually, using their own skills and individually possessed assets' (Bauman, 2008:4). Neoliberal economics is based on the idea of the autarkic self; it takes for granted that humans are self-sufficient and devising their own lives on their own. The promotion of self-sufficiency conflicts with everyday experiences in the family, at school and at work; individuals are no nomads and deliberately are tied to others in their everyday life in their mutual obligation.

David Harvey (2005), a leading exponent of the history of neoliberalism, has provided a thorough and sensible analysis of the penetration of liberalization not only in the West, but also in China and India. Harvey's global neoliberalism is defined as the renewal of free-market economic policy and in terms of how it gained momentum in its rapid diffusion around the world, having in the process significant social-structural and cultural consequences;

its influence witnessed by growing deregulation and privatization. It is a system based on universal competition which relies on a framework of assessment and monitoring, designed to identify winners and losers. The inequality in the distribution of wealth grew rapidly with rising rents, privatization and deregulation. The economist and political philosopher Friedrich von Hayek (1899–1992), the brain behind the circuit of ideas of neoliberalism, warned against the road to socialism while praising the virtues of the open society and open market in *The Road to Serfdom* (1944). Hayek's liberalism, influential in Britain especially during the 1970s, was put to practice by reacting against the macro-economic theories of Keynes as part of the neoliberal agenda by giving priority to inflation control before unemployment measures and minimizing state intervention in the market (Yergin and Stanislaw, 1998). The ideas of Milton Friedman, who wrote 'the rulebook for the contemporary hypermobile global economy' (Klein, 2007:4), supported *laissez-faire* economics and the diminished authority of the state in economic affairs. Free markets, free trade and the minimal role of the government, protecting only the civil freedom of individual, are key factors of the neoliberal ideology. For Friedman (1962), the days of government intervention in private affairs would disappear. Countries like the UK and America adopted these free-market policies creating a new environment by shifting public policy to strategize along free-market principles. Companies have the potential to move their registered offices to more advantageous locations around the world. The advantageous locations are those that offer the lowest rates of taxation, a cheap workforce and the least regulated employment laws (Gorz, 1999).

It is worth noting here that neoliberalism is not a unitary notion; it is more of a set of loosely related ideas with different origins and trajectories. Their convergence lies in the focus on the individual rather than on society as a whole and that its agenda rests on the fact that the best practice for economic progress is to give free rein to market forces. Neoliberal thinking equates to a profit motive in which all aspects of social life have to be justified in utilitarian terms with claims that individualized, market competition is superior to other forms of organization. Neoliberalism has been approached mainly as an overarching hegemonic global discourse (Bourdieu, 1998, Harvey, 2005). More recent works are now cagey of this hegemonic conceptualization and examine the glocal variations of neoliberalism in different locations (Freeman, 2007, Gershon, 2011) as well as in counter-hegemonic discourses (Morgan and Gonzales, 2008).

In view of the conceptual looseness of neoliberalism, as 'a phenomenon which manifests itself everywhere and in everything' (Gamble, 2001:134), it is often seen as 'imprecise and over-used' (Watkins, 2010:7); herein, I follow David Harvey's definition of neoliberalism as

> a theory of political economic practices that proposed that human well-being can be best advanced by liberating individual entrepreneurial freedoms and skills within an institutional framework characterized by strong private property rights, free markets, and free trade. (Harvey, 2005:2)

The interest in this book is to make sense of the subjectivity of neoliberalism. By this subjectivity I am referring to Ilana Gershon's (2011) concept of the neoliberalism of agency and applying it to the lives of millennials in southern Europe. This book is concerned with the social organization and epistemological differences of southern European countries compared to the Anglo-American context. Rigorous analysis of social organization is crucial in the retort to neoliberal discourse which often regards individuals as a corporate bunch of autonomous persons.

Central questions of the book

The central questions of this book are the following:

> How is the Anglo-American individualized lifestyle adopted and adapted in southern Europe?
> What are the financial and emotional burdens of millennials today?
> How are the networks of cooperation in the South cushioning these burdens?

Even though the educational system, its workings and shifts to fit in with a more neoliberal climate are considerably explored in this book, it is not its sole focus. The previous editions within this book series had done this brilliantly. This book fits in this series by presenting an in-depth exploration of the actual lived experiences of millennials with tertiary education, their sense of control in their life decisions and their apprehensions and life chances as graduates experiencing individualized neoliberal risks. As a response to the expansion and extension of the educational system, most of these young persons are the first generation to go to university, the first to exhibit middle-class angst of being in ambivalent class position. What's more, they are experiencing struggles to prove themselves in a competitive environment. Specifically, this book explores the structure of feelings for this particular generation.

Organization of content

The chapters of the book are theoretical and conceptual in character. Chapter 1 is about the extension and expansion of the educational system since the 1960s within the Anglo-American and the southern European context, framed within recent socio-economic shifts. It explores the expansion of the educational system and its implications on the conceptualization of youth itself as a transitional life course. The expansion and extension of the educational system were one decisive element in the longevity of youth as a stage of dependence. Discourse on social mobility, as one of the consequences of the increased access to higher education, is equally given considerable importance in this chapter.

Chapter 2 builds on this by exploring the increased importance placed on credentials in tandem with the neoliberal economy. This is followed by making sense of the financial implications of extending years in education, framed within the climate of academic capitalism. It explores the upward-credentialization and educational inflation as part of the reality of millennials. This chapter also takes into consideration the rise in financial hardship as an outcome of the growth in conspicuous consumption and its influence on the normalization of debts.

Chapter 3 examines institutional changes in the school to work transition, shifts in job opportunities and patterns of unemployment – all having a direct impact on youth's transitional stages into adulthood. It puts attention on the workforce as being increasingly 'flexible', with a decline in a career-long mode of employment and the rise in contingent job contracts. This situation is quite at odds with the social reality of younger people during the 1960s within the Anglo-American context. This chapter traces the trajectories of these shifts.

Chapter 4 explores the consequences of the embodiment of a neoliberal application on the self. It deals with the influence of neoliberalism on subjectivity and how millennials have been immersed into this mode of thinking as a 'natural' way of doing things and seeing the world around them. In tandem with the shifts from state responsibility onto the individual and the dismantling of the welfare state and its safety nets, individuals are more than ever responsible for their own success and failures. The chapter explores this kind of embodiment of neoliberalism on the self for millennials by understanding transversal feelings of anxiety, resentment, pessimism as well as tendencies for self-reliance, perfectionism and self-entrepreneurship.

The last three chapters focus squarely on the specificities of the southern context.

Chapter 5 unpacks the cultural cushioning system in southern Europe and explores how this eases the transition from youth into adulthood. Explicitly, this chapter looks at the family network, kinship patterns and cultural conditions in traditional families in southern European countries like Italy, Spain, Portugal and Malta and make sense of how these function as 'shock-absorbers', cushioning members from short-term deprivations like unemployment and family breakdown.

Chapter 6 specifically focuses on one southern European country, the Maltese islands, to address the typical implications of cultural, historical and socio-economic conditions which in return substantially shape the life experiences of young people. Despite the differences in economic realities of Malta with other southern European countries, Malta is referred to here as one exemplary case of how it has adapted, at a different speed to other southern countries, to broader European socio-economic systems. Compared to other western locations, economic developments as well as the individualization process were 'delayed' in ex-colonial locations like Malta, which tended to be late in the processes of socio-economic and cultural changes compared to other western European countries. The chapter explores Malta's economic development and how it reached a surge in the last four decades, with the development of the welfare state, the national health services and the implementation of subsidized housing.

Part of my discussion in these chapters is conceptual but the last chapter is also empirical. This chapter builds on the previous chapter on the social, historical, economic and cultural conditions of southern Europe's smallest country by drawing from the outcomes of a qualitative study conducted on the life situations of tertiary-educated millennials in Malta. Qualitative citations were selected for this chapter to reflect typical patterns of responses of youth who were transitioning from full-time education to their first full-time jobs during the time of the interview between the years 2010 and 2012. Despite the small sample size, it does give an indication on the meanings and feelings of some of these youth, particularly on their strategies of negotiation and accommodation of cultural circumstances with their individualized lifestyle. It discussed the notion of 'compromised choices' on how youths attempt to strike a balance between their willingness to gratify cultural norms and their desires of designing their own life plan.

On southern Europe

The southern European region has an enthralling blend of diverse cultures. Yet, there are specific cultural commonalities that warrant exploration and explanation. These include the region's kinship bonds of clientelism and patronage, religious legitimation of public institutions generating consent over the masses and their post-colonial or post right-wing authoritarian regimes in the last century of some of these southern European countries.

It is worth questioning whether commonalities in the south are the outcome of cultural affinity or common socio-economic circumstances. Central questions in the design of this book, particularly in the process of sketching out its aims, were: Is it a question of validating some form of modernization theory in the South where economic development, socio-political change and cultural change come together in a coherent and to some extent predictable fashion? Or is it about assuming that the southern European region is to be understood in terms of a delayed or 'slower motion' modernization? To illuminate such questions and analyse them in contrast to the Anglo-American context, it was necessary to explore the peculiarities, tendencies and values upheld in the southern region.

In the last three decades, various southern European researchers have addressed these issues in relation to historical and policy traits in the South and stressed the shared commonalities of this region (Esping-Andersen, 1990, Ferrera, 1996). Predominantly, they put weight on the southern politico-institutional dynamics derived from distinctive welfare arrangements and the typical 'Mediterranean' response to challenges as well as the centrality of the familialism in the provision of welfare. While recognizing that the family has changed in form and function over the last few decades in southern European countries, yet in general, precedence is still attributed to strong kinship ties and the institutionalization of marriage (Cliquet, 2003, Viazzo, 2010). Specifically, family networks remain central in assuming obligations and responsibility in care for intergenerational relations and in the way the family organizes support for its members, what David Sven Reher (1998) refers to as the 'strong' family ties of the Mediterranean southern European region as compared to 'weak' ties in northern countries. In Italy, for example, parents are traditionally assumed to be deeply involved in the lives and decisions of their adult children, including in their choices on marriage and cohabitation (Di Giulio and Rosina, 2007). It is also the case that 'children ... avoid choices which openly clash with the values of parents' (Rosina and Fraboni, 2004:162).

The centrality of the family and kinship networks has a substantial impact on the understanding of the functioning of the welfare state. The conservative welfare regime, typical in southern Europe, contrasts with the kind of welfare model in other European countries (Esping-Andersen, 1990). Such peculiarities in all aspects of social life, addressed in this book, give light to the dissimilarity in the application of processes, such as those related to the degree of individualization and the 'spirit' of neoliberalism, partly the result of the 'delay' in economic development in post-colonial countries. Their 'take-off' (Rostow, 1960) stage of development process was 'delayed' compared to other western European countries for various factors which are addressed in this book.

On economic levels, southern European countries share similar characteristics typical of peripheral or semi-peripheral economies with tenacious productivity, competitiveness and educational deficits. Having exports based on medium-to-low added value products and non-transactional goods, such countries are more prone to vulnerability to the contingencies of the business cycle and international trade deregulation (Sebastião et al., 2013).

On political levels, there are some similarities in the recent political history of these states. In the last century, countries like Portugal, Spain, Greece and Italy share relatively recent experiences of right-wing authoritarian regimes: Franco in Spain, Salazar in Portugal, Mussolini in Italy and the Metaxas dictatorship and the colonels' regime in Greece. In Portugal, the forty years of fascism had profound effects on economic, social and cultural development. The joining of the European Community for Greece, Spain and Portugal in the 1980s was a step towards democratic systems. In exchange for financial assistance, since 2009, the European Union had encouraged southern European countries to implement a political agenda of austerity to reduce debt; Greeks and Portuguese, Spaniards and Italians suffered major cuts in household income, resulting in widening the gap between the rich and the poor and engendering new forms of inequality. Consequentially, the World Bank estimate Gini index, a measure of statistical dispersion of the income or wealth distribution of a nation's residents, went from an average of 29 in the year 2000 to 30.6 in 2012, having the south of Europe experiencing the highest levels (Kapoor and Coller, 2014). In Spain, it went up to 36.2 in 2015, Greece 36, Italy 35.4, Portugal 35.5 and Malta 29.4 (The World Bank, 2019).

On environmental and cultural levels, several studies have dealt with the link between climate and social behaviour. Principally, Fernand Braudel (1996) studied how the economic, social and political life of Mediterranean societies was strongly influenced by the seasons: in particular, the two distinct seasons of summer, as a dry period stretching between April and October and the wet and stormy winter period. Summer is characterized by activity; tourism, communal rituals and traditional religious events and celebrations of community patron saints take place in summer. The increase in summer entertainment heightens the summer relaxation mode.

Southern European societies are also subject to divergences, including in the uneven stages of economic development and in their highly and increasingly heterogeneous ethnic and cultural mix. For this reason, it is naïve to rank southern European countries under one classification of societies as opposed to more Anglo-American generalizations: familiar backwardness versus post-modernity, traditional fatalism versus individualism, religious mentality versus rationalism. Yet still, in view of certain peculiarities, including common geopolitical and cultural conditions, it is safe to talk about the area with restricted generalizations (Giner, 1982). Nonetheless, the applicability of the individualized lifestyle mode investigated here can be applied to any other given location that is also in ambivalence between modernity and tradition.

On youth

> House prices are too expensive, flights are too cheap and relationships are far more complex. [...] Why have a child when you can have a dog. [...] There is no way I am moving out of my parent's at the moment. (24-year-old, university student, living in Malta)

The focus of this book is on young adults, more specifically highly educated youth with tertiary level education. I have a personal stake in the matter. I have a particular interest in life histories of young people and on how they reflect on their lives and understand their own everyday experiences. I focused my doctoral dissertation on this, especially when during the time, I could consider myself as 'an insider' to this situation – a PhD student, with little form of stability in all aspects of life. I consider myself fortunate enough to have carried out my PhD studies in the UK before 'austerity measures' were in place tripling tuition fees in 2010. If I hadn't done so, it would have been daunting to face monthly payments to pay off my student loan for a number of my adult years.

Despite efforts to be as objective as possible in my doctoral study, I cannot ignore the fact that this study was in part autobiographical. My own experiences played a crucial role especially in choosing this field for research. Yet, despite being very much aware that a value-neutral study cannot be completely obtained, as famously maintained by Max Weber (1949[1904]), the acquisition of a sociological imagination has presented me with an opportunity to be a stranger within my own territory, within my own generation.

Born in the early 1980s, I gradually grew more conscious of my life situation and often questioned what I wanted to get out of life. I was brought up and trained in a rather conservative location in southern Europe where the collective sentiments and moral constraints were still robust, along with the importance given to kinship ties. It was during my university years that I felt at the crossroad to choose a path that would presumably lead me to a 'stable' job, with sufficient earnings to maintain a socially accepted standard of living. It was also during this time that I decided to buy my own place. It felt natural to consider taking a bank loan, tying me to a repayment schedule for the next forty years – a normal rite of passage of young people today, who are pursuing their independence. Since my doctoral years, I am looking at the situation more as an 'outsider', not only because I passed the age-bracket categorization of youth, but also because I landed different sorts of responsibilities in my life that tie me more to the life stage of adulthood.

Today, in my everyday life as a university lecturer, I face a number of young adults, the more or less privileged ones who have opportunities and access to tertiary education. More often than not, they are a bag of nerves, uncertain about their studies, their job prospects and of all the apprehensions that transitioning into adulthood brings – surely a situation that is not only tied to the millennials but to any youth generation in transit.

Building on Michael Pickering's (2008) observations on the purposes of applying cultural studies, in studying millennials, I am very much interested in the subjective dimension of social relation and explore how social arrangements and configurations are lived by this generation and made sense of. In doing so, it is inevitable to pinpoint the complex intersectional dynamics between public culture and private subjectivity of these youth.

This book makes reference to millennials as a generation, not to explicitly focus on age categorization but rather to link specific economic and social structures during a particular period of time with one's identity and biography. Millennials are roughly those individuals born between 1980 and 1995, thus ranging from those who will turn forty in 2020 to those who will be twenty-five years old. Clearly, the fifteen-year age difference is worth taking into consideration because it has extensive impact on whether someone is still pursuing tertiary education and doing part-time casual work in their twenties, compared to those who are more likely to have a full-time job and starting a family in their late thirties. With this in mind, it is too naïve to categorize them as a homogeneous generation. Yet, what I am more interested is to have an understanding of these young adults who share a particular culture of a period; they were all born in what has been referred to as a 'risk society' by Ulrich Beck

(1992) and Anthony Giddens (1991) – by which it refers to the intensification of manufactured risks in modernity and the shift from traditional securities to individuals shouldering responsibilities for their own security. These shifts are more likely to obfuscate millennials in their lived experiences compared to their predecessors.

Dubbed as 'snowflakes' for their presumed sheltered over-nurtured upbringing as well as the 'Me Me Me Generation' by Joel Stein in *Time* magazine in 2013, millennials are caricatured as having narcissistic personalities. They are considered for setting high expectations and are fame-obsessed.

To define a generation accurately, I draw from the work of Karl Mannheim (1952) who referred to a generation not simply in relation to an age cohort but to people who lived through the same historical period and experiences that influenced their attitudes, values and behaviour. In view of this, throughout this book I refer to millennials as a generation in terms of the interplay between specific historical moments and economic fluctuations on life biographies. People who live through the same period of time, albeit their different life chances due to, amongst others, class and/or ethnic background, tend to develop a shared set of outlooks, values and beliefs throughout their 'biological rhythm of life' (Mannheim, 1952:290). In a similar yet more recent sociological definition, McCrindle and Wolfinger (2010) regarded a generation as 'a group of people born in the same era, shaped by the same times and influenced by the same social markers; in other words, a cohort united by age and life stage, conditions and technology, events and experiences' (2010:19). The division of generations in society in this regard is done by subjective sociological measurements that are based not on particular markers but more on social demographics. To take this further, the last century can be classified as having four main distinctive generations: the Silent Generation 1928–1945, the Baby Boomers 1946–1964, Generation X 1965–1980 and Millennials 1980–2000.

The age at which one is exposed to political shifts and technological change is considered as an important factor because it determines the extent to which such events and crisis are embedded in one's psyche and worldviews (McCrindle and Wolfinger, 2010). People develop a form of collective identity separating them from preceding generations. Nevertheless, it is not correct to ascribe universal attributes to a generation and assume that a youth generation living during the same time had the same characteristics, irrespective of the cultural particularities of its location.

In making sense of the generation of millennials with tertiary education, I felt it was inevitable to compare it to another generation and address generational differences, especially within the field of education and the labour market. The so-called 'baby boom' generation, born around 1945 and who are now in their 'third age' life stage, are referred to in relation to the political, economic and social situation in the last sixty years. The aftermath of the Second World War marks a momentous time of sweeping social, economic, technological and cultural changes in recent history, with the dissolving of traditional hierarchies making way to the birth of a modern age. It is not the scope of this book to document the vast changes unleashed during the last six decades. Nonetheless, references to economic changes are unavoidable to contextualize changes in youth's life chances. Various chapters in this book give prominence to contextual changes in the lived experiences of highly educated youth by providing a socio-economic and cultural framework.

The generational polarities today are more extreme than ever: the millenarians versus the baby-boomers, the age of austerity versus the 'golden age'. It bears much truth to say that there is a common pattern of change in the life situation of Anglo-American youth since the post-Second World War: from a traditional structured transition into adulthood embedded in a conservative communal society to more individualized trajectories constrained by new demands from the educational system and the job market. It became conventional wisdom that millennials are the 'worse-off' youth generation compared to its predecessors, who on the contrary 'never had it as good'. Yet, it is also true that millennials are more than ever cutting through global, cultural and socio-economic boundaries when compared to previous youth generations. They are more formally educated and technologically proficient. They are also more logged on and linked up through the cyber world.

Herein, it is important to also note how the first decade of the new millennium was a period particularly notable for the intensification of globalization, as a form of capitalist reorganization, not just in the economic sphere but in the everyday life of individuals. The process of globalization greatly influences the way people communicate, work and process knowledge (Lieber and Weisberg, 2002, Schirato and Webb, 2003).

This book also aims to problematize the Anglo-American economic scenario and the generational inequity between the working generation and those retired, living off publicly funded pensions. The main argument is centred on the fact that the working population is funding the pensions of today's elderly while they are not guaranteed welfare security for their own retirement. Older persons today are said to be taking far more than their fair share, leaving young people paying for their well-being without having any financial security themselves. A growing polarization amongst the future retired population is predicted as a consequence of schemes implemented on contemporary workers. The heavy reliance on the labour market for the provision of welfare in old age has to be supported by relatively stable full-time employment for the accumulation of such funds. Failing to provide high and secure wages and offering short-term contract or precarious employment instead are the cause for future inequalities and disturbances in the life course, especially later on in life.

Yet, irrespective of their differences, both generations have shared certain similarities as youth. For this highly educated social group, common events lead to their transition from dependence to independence, including studying and finding a middle-class job, becoming financially independent, leaving their parental home and family formation. Yet, the structural and cultural factors of a location play out an important role in when and how these societal rites of passage unfold.

Overnight, the infamous avocado toast became a symbol of ambivalence for the well-educated millennials who seem to have troubles prioritizing their finances. This begs a number of questions. Should we leave out the added financial constraints in the process of obtaining a degree or two within a neoliberal climate of self-reliance? Should we ignore the family network supporting youth? Are students really navigating their own life plans effortlessly on their own free-will and shouldering anxiety single-handed? Can we ignore the safety net in the South that is at times cushioning youth? My firm belief to these questions is a resounding no. This book digs further into this.

1

The extension and expansion of education

For the last six decades, the expansion of the educational systems was directed towards a form of social levelling to equalize opportunities and enable children from deprived backgrounds to prosper. Policy changes in education were in place to provide assurance for pupils from low-income backgrounds to be given opportunities for intergenerational social mobility. But some studies point to the opposite direction – children coming from deprived backgrounds are still ill-equipped to climb the social ladder (Bourdieu 1973, Bowles and Gintis, 1976, Willis, 1977). In view of this, scholars wrote about the opportunity gaps between those who have opportunities for higher education compared to those who don't, predominantly based on their ethnic background, gender and/or the annual household income.

Instead of building on this body of study, my focus in this chapter is to sketch out the shifts in the educational system and explore their implications on those who have had opportunities for tertiary education. This is worth considering in view of the overall aim of this book to provide an understanding of youth with tertiary education; these amount to 34.2 per cent of those aged twenty-five to fifty-four years in the EU28, with some southern European countries score at the lowest scale: Italy (20.6 per cent), Malta (24.4 per cent) and Portugal (27.6 per cent) (Eurostat, 2017).

This chapter starts off by setting the framework for exploring the recent shifts in the educational system in the last sixty years or so, within the Anglo-American context by referring to the British educational reforms as an exemplary case. It also examines such shifts within the southern European context by looking at policy changes and the implementation of legislation that facilitated the opening up of the educational system and resulted in greater opportunities for social mobility. Prior to elaborating on the educational system, it is essential to mention the recent changes in the actual conceptualization of youth itself, in part as a result of these shifts in education. It is no doubt that the expansion and extension of the educational system were one decisive element in the longevity of youth as a stage of dependence.

Conceptualizing youth

The timings of different life stages and the conceptualization of youth are very much shaped by the time spent in education – the longer one is a full-time student, the more she/he usually delays transitioning into adulthood. As a life course adulthood is often measured in terms of financial independence and leaving parental home. Yet, life courses have become fuzzy today with changes in individuals' biographical timetables. Youth are less likely to follow the traditional socially expected and culturally transmitted age-norms.

Irrespective of this, there are still transversal traits in youths' transitions. Puberty marks the start of the consciousness of sex and its expression: the beginning of intimate relationships and the training phase preparing for adulthood. The anthropologist Arnold Van Gennep (1960) identified the ritual ceremonies manifesting life-course transitions in his account on the rites of passage. He explored the age-related social transitions of individuals, celebrated by ritual practices that promote stability in society:

> The life of an individual in any society is a series of passages from one age to another. For every one of these events there are ceremonies whose essential purpose is to enable the individual to pass from one defined position to another. (Van Gennep, 1960:2–3)

Especially in 'primitive' societies – by which I am referring to tribal societies based on stages of early settlement and the degree of technological and social organizational complexity – rites of passage display how the individual becomes detached from the previous stage and passes through an intermediary state until incorporating the new set of rules, roles and obligations of the successive social position. An individual in transition is considered to move from one life stage to another in three phases: the rituals that mark the separation from one life stage to another, the liminality of being moved to another stage and finally the incorporation into the new life stage (Van Gennep, 1960).

In recent years, youth transitions are comparable, according to Zygmunt Bauman (1996) in 'From Pilgrim to Tourist', to the experiences of a 'tourist'. Just like the journey of a pilgrim, the formation of identity in the past had an ultimate plan to reach the goal. Yet in postmodern society, the route towards adulthood resembles more that of tourists, having a clear awareness of the goal, but individuals may simply decide to go places for new experiences before reaching such goals. This shift crystallizes the changes in youth's biographical patterns.

The trends summarized by the terms extensions, destandardization, fragmentation and individualization of the life course vary in their intensity between societies and social groups. Speaking on the delay in life-course transitions, there are numerous studies on the increased fluidity of social boundaries separating life-course stages and delays in the life-course transition into adulthood (Arnett, 2000, 2004, 2006, Chisholm, 1995, Clark, 2007). Chisholm (1995) empirically proved from his numerous studies carried out in western and southern Europe that the contemporary youth phase has extended further compared to the past:

> The social boundaries between life course phases are more fluid than they used to be. Quite simply, the trends summarised by the terms extensions, destandardisation, fragmentation and individualisation of the life course are not in dispute, although their intensity varies between societies and social groups. (Chisholm, 1995:127)

Primarily, it is worth understanding who is considered as youth. Youth as a definitive autonomous stage of life gained its prominence in the mid-twentieth century particularly with the emergence of the social category 'teenager' (Savage, 2008). There is no doubt that opportunities for higher education and full employment were distinguishing factors for the creation of 'teenager' as a distinctive age in most of western Europe during the 1960s. It is said that young people in the West experienced the expansion and extension of education, which had a direct bearing on their advantageous life chances (Hobsbawn, 1996).

Warren Clark (2007) maintained that the timing of transitions has been delayed since the 1970s. He identified five main factors for such delay in youth's transition into adulthood. These are shifts in leaving school, moving out of the parental home, having a full-year full-time work, entering conjugal relationships and having children. When comparing data from the census, he found that typical 25-year-olds in 2001 have made the same number of transitions as 22-year-olds in 1971.

Observations on such delays have led Jeffrey Jensen Arnett (2000, 2006) to come up with a new separate phase of 'emerging adulthood'. Arnett (2006) disputed the conceptualization of youth as the intermediate phase between childhood and adulthood by saying that

> youth is too vague and elastic a term to be useful in describing the new and unprecedented period that now lies after adolescence but before full adulthood ... Any word that is intended to be applied to people in the entire age range from 10 to 12 until at least 25 cannot possibly work, because the typical 10 or 12 or 15 or 17 year-old is simply too different from the typical 25-year-old. (Arnett, 2006:119)

Arnett (2006) maintained that the term 'young adulthood' is no longer suitable to describe youth who are in their twenties. Instead, the term 'emerging adulthood' should be used. Many people in their twenties do not subjectively define themselves as adults, and therefore for Arnett, the term 'young adulthood' is misleading as it implies that youth define themselves as such. Because of the extension between the stages of youth and adulthood, individuals are extending the time of enjoying, not having full adult responsibility yet at the same time being semi-autonomous.

Arnett's (2006) proposal of this new concept of youth is characterized by identity exploration, trying out new possibilities in love and work, instability, self-focus and the feeling in between adolescence and adulthood. In this liminal stage of 'emerging adulthood', young people free themselves from the normative expectations of childhood dependency and move into exploring the variety of possible life directions. In their early twenties, young people tend to be more committed to move out of the family home, establish stable relationships and choose their adult identity. However, typically they do not regard themselves as adults but more as individuals making long-term commitments and decisions (Arnett, 2006). Because of the postponement of full independence because of extending the years in full-time education, adulthood is assumed to be reached around the age of thirty.

Yet, Arnett's (2000, 2006) new conceptualization is viewed with scepticism. Bynner and Côté (2008) found little reason to view 'emerging adulthood' as a new developmental period. Instead, they argued that support of this new concept comes from those who simply want a useful metaphor to make sense of changes in the transitions of youth to adulthood. They stated that they were not convinced that

> the developmental necessities for the transition to adulthood have changed fundamentally and thus that a new developmental phase of the life-course has been established that potentially applied to all young people. (Bynner and Côté, 2008:252)

Various studies referred to the shifts in youth by assuming that Anglo-American youths in the 1960s were brought up with a more organized life plan cemented in traditional social structures (Ashton and Field, 1976, Coles, 1995, Kohli, 1996, Mills and Blossfeld, 2001, Furlong and Cartmel, 2007[1997]), whereas individuals experiencing their youth in recent years have more autonomy when devising their own biography (Giddens, 1991, Beck, 1994, Bauman, 1996, Beck and Beck-Gernsheim, 2008[2002]).

It warrants to mention that the concept of 'emerging adulthood' 'exists only in cultures which allow young people a prolonged period of independent role exploration during the late teens and twenties' (Arnett, 2000:469). Yet still, Arnett did not explain what causes the variations of those who experience such developmental stage and those who do not (Bynner and Côté, 2008). Based on their observations, Bynner and Côté (2008) concluded that the conceptualization of the life stage described as 'emerging adulthood' fails to recognize the population heterogeneity including marginalized youth as well as structural components influencing one's life-course transition. In this regard, the study on youth cannot be understood divorced from one's social positioning.

An understanding of youths' actions is perceived as being the product of both dispositions and reflexive decisions. Despite the noteworthy difference in the approaches of both the concept of habitus and studies on human agency,

Elder-Vass (2007) accentuated that the two can be reconciled into a single theory. In particular, he maintained that the work of Bourdieu (1990) on the social conditioning determining behaviour and Margaret Archer's (2000, 2003) stress on reflexive choices can be reconciled with some modification. Human action is essentially the outcome of continuous interaction between dispositions and reflexivity (Elder-Vass, 2007).

It is an undeniable fact that youths' biographies are very much embedded in its context. It is not only a question of individual agency, but structural factors play an equally important part. Norbert Elias (2000[1939]) emphasized the importance of one's habitus as a constituent part of what makes the individual's life chances and dispositions. For Elias, childhood is the main 'transmission belt' for the development of the habitus.

> It is the web of social relations in which individuals live during their most impressionable phase, that is childhood and youth, which imprints itself upon their unfolding personality in the form of the relationship between their controlling agencies, super-ego and ego and their libidinal impulses. The resulting balance ... determines how an individual person steers him or herself in his or her social relations with others ... However, there is no end to the intertwining. (Elias, 2000[1939]:377)

Biographies are considered the product of 'the particular family living in a house situated in a certain area' (Pollock, 2002:69). Youths' identities are formed and reformed by structures and experiences. This makes sense when focusing on millennials with tertiary education as a social group of youth who were born in a family that is culturally and economically supportive of their post-compulsory education.

Changes in the educational system in the last sixty years

'Education, not nationalisation, was to be the main engine in the creation of a more just society' (Crosland, 1982:69). Education, as a fundamental human right, recognized as one of the pillars of the economic system was attributed meticulous attention during the second half of the twentieth century. The scholar Eric Hobsbawn, who shaped the global Marxist imagination in the twentieth century, wrote methodically on how the opening up of the educational system and the provision of full employment had significant implications on youths' life-course transitions within the socio-economic context of the post-Second World War. In his book *The Age of Extremes*, he wrote about how socio-economic, political and cultural changes between 1950s and the early 1970s made this period 'golden'. The affluence of this period manifested itself in better standards of living 'for all'. Equipped with historical analysis, Hobsbawn (1996) explained the accumulated advantages of youth during these years. People's life chances are said to have improved substantially with the expansion of the educational system and measures in place to minimize poverty. In assessing the 'goldenness' of this period, Hobsbawn gave credit to the Keynesian combination of economic growth in a capitalist economy based on mass consumption of a fully employed, well-paid and well-protected labour force.

The period following the Second World War brought institutional stability at a time when welfare was considered a fundamental feature of western statehood (Hobsbawn, 1996, Kus, 2006). The Bretton Woods agreement that controlled the international economy and considered to be 'the backbone of post-war embedded liberalism' (Kus, 2006:492) accentuated the common realities amongst western European countries during the post-war period.

State intervention and the increase in the social wage guaranteed full-time stable employment especially for young people. Up until the 1980s, having no academic qualifications did not hinder you from finding work in places such as Britain; the labour market virtually absorbed everyone, and opportunities for the unqualified and unskilled were easily available (Bynner and Côté, 2008). Notwithstanding the various divergences in policy implementation of educational reforms in countries in the West, Britain is referred to here as an example of how the development in the educational system, geared towards a meritocratic system, was arguably promoting social mobility for all.

This so-called post-war consensus, fuelled by the application of John Maynard Keynes, whose work as an economist was based on post-war settlement, resulted in full employment and the development of public services working as safety nets 'from cradle to grave'. Keynes had advocated strong government intervention in order to manage markets. Such measures also brought institutional stability, mainly reflected in the advantageous life chances experienced by youth at a time when the welfare provisions were a fundamental feature of western statehood.

The Keynesian economics aimed at the well-being of all classes by providing a welfare system for the inclusion of everyone as a way forward out of the severe downturn in economic activity during the interwar period. Similar to other western European countries, Britain's social legislation in the immediate post-war years was focused on combating the 'Five Giants' – want, disease, squalor, ignorance and idleness (Jones, 2005[2000]). The 'Social Insurance and Allied Services' report by the economist William Beveridge was the blueprint for the state to take responsibility for the well-being of its citizens (Yergin and Stanislaw, 1998):

> The Plan for Social Security is designed to secure, by a comprehensive scheme of social insurance, that every individual, on conditions of working while he can and contributing from his earnings, shall have an income sufficient for the healthy subsistence of himself and his family. (Beveridge, 1944:17)

It is certainly clear that young people benefitted directly from changes in measures aimed at combating 'ignorance' and inducing mass participation in higher education in the British education system. Students coming from different social backgrounds benefitted directly from policies implemented to open the doors to higher education (Heath, 2003). Moreover, policies based on the principle of equality of opportunity offered student support grants. The real concern of the 1944 'Education Act' in Britain was the promotion of educational opportunity for all pupils under a unified system of free compulsory schooling between the ages of five and fifteen.

The eleven-plus exam, introduced in this Education Act, intended to channel pupils into state secondary schools geared to their abilities. However, when Anthony Crosland became Secretary of State for Education between 1964 and 1970, he worked for the abolition of this exam in an attempt to facilitate greater equality of opportunity and promote social mobility (Fenwick, 1976).

The commitment to free education intended to maximize the number of students with higher education. For instance, in 1956 the Anderson Committee offered student support grants to reach those with financial difficulties, based on the principle of equality of opportunity. This was followed by the so-called 'Robbins Report', aimed at enhancing the educational opportunities for many young people in 1963 by committing the government to increase students in higher education by 50 per cent in four years and by 250 per cent in 1980 (Dunford and Sharp, 1990). These actions led to a large expansion in the number of university students and university institutions. Actions were also carried out with the intention to develop an all-inclusive educational system. The increase in polytechnics ensured that those students who did not qualify for universities had the opportunity to follow courses up to a degree level (Lawton, 2004). The White paper in Britain 'A Plan for Polytechnics and Other Colleges' published by Crosland in 1966 was designed to create or upgrade a number of LEA (Local Education Authority) Colleges to higher education standards. Despite these measures for the promotion of meritocratic principles to encourage students to enter into higher education, gender, class and ethnic inequalities still persisted and remained determining factors in one's educational career (Bourdieu 1973, Bowles and Gintis, 1976, Willis, 1977).

How did this all change?

The rift between those who could attend higher education and those who could not became wider with the collapse of Keynesian policies on both sides of the Atlantic by the 1970s. Further inequalities in educational opportunities became apparent with cuts in public funding in most countries in Western societies, as a direct measure of neoliberal government policies. The privatization of public services brought about changes in the fund allocations for education.

Neoliberal strategies in educational reforms in the last few decades were similar to those measures that guided economic and social welfare (Apple, 2004). Such comparisons include the added stress to expand the free market, reduce government responsibility for funding and reinforce competitive structures at school. These reforms popularized a form of Social-Darwinist thinking, as the book by Richard Herrnstein and Charles Murray (1994) *Bell Curve* worryingly indicate on the nature of inequalities and family background.

Principally predominant in the last two decades, educational reforms aimed at commodifying public education by compartmentalizing learning into categories of information and marketized them through programmes that promote privatization. Congruently, neoliberal education reform policies focus on high-stakes 'accountability', measurement and management strategies to reward or penalize students' performance.

In a free-market and its promise to offer freedom of choice, people are said to have the power to choose between different options in all social transactions. With increased emphasis on competition between educational institutions, students and their parents feel they have a choice in finding the best school, while schools feel they have to 'sell themselves' in the market of competition. In this way, neoliberal reforms promote the right to choose schools for parents and students rather than have students attend a zoned school. Consequently, students living in poor and low-income neighbourhoods do not have such choice, resulting in further segregation and inequalities. This was evident in a recent study on the changes in inequalities and patterns of segregation in New York high schools during a period of neoliberal reforms between 2000 and 2013 (Brathwaite, 2017).

Southern European countries are particularly badly hit by neoliberal moves in the economic situation. The welfare state in countries in the South suffered a blow with reforms and cuts in public expenditure on education as a percentage of gross domestic product (GDP) in countries like Italy (3.9 per cent) and Spain (4 per cent), below the European Union (EU) average of 4.6 per cent in 2017 (Eurostat, 2019a).

Changes in the educational system in southern Europe

Low economic activity, high unemployment and low consumption in southern European countries have had symptomatic effects on deficits in education and training, especially in the last decade during and after the economic recession. In the last few decades, the share of highly educated individuals has steadily increased in Europe despite still falling short of figures in the United States. In southern Europe, statistics on education remain below the average EU. The European Commission Report *Education and Training Monitor* (European Commission, 2018) refers to the fact that some southern European countries still have the highest levels of early school-leavers in the European Union, with Spain at 18.3 per cent, Portugal at 12.6 per cent and Italy at 14 per cent in comparison to the EU average of 10.6 per cent. It also follows that such countries have the lowest rates of persons with tertiary education – Italy at 26.9 per cent and Portugal at 33.5 per cent (European Commission, 2018). In view of this, the European Commission, as part of the strategic framework for European cooperation in education and training, set a political agenda to increase the number of tertiary-educated individuals to at least 40 per cent by 2020. National economic, political crises and austere measures in countries like Greece, Italy, Portugal and Spain had direct effect on policymaking and funding in education in the south.

Recent reforms were introduced to improve the quality of teaching, including new school and teacher evaluation systems, in places like Italy, and a new funding formula linked to performance criteria in Portugal. Spain introduced school reforms, including newly designed curriculum, assessment system and promotion of skill-based teaching and learning (Romei, 2016). Malta is also investing heavily in education and training to improve learning outcomes and tackle the challenge of the high rate of early school leavers and the low rate of persons in tertiary education. Its general expenditure, as a proportion of total public expenditure (14.1 per cent in 2016), is well above the EU averages (10.2 per cent) (European Commission, 2018). In Malta, development of the education sector is guided by the *Framework for the Education Strategy* for 2014 to 2024. The objectives for this ten-year period are to

> reduce the gender gap in educational outcomes and the gap between students attending different schools, and increase overall attainment; Support educational achievement of children at risk of poverty and from low socio-economic status, and reduce Early School Leaving; Increase participation in lifelong learning and adult learning; Raise attainment levels in Further and Higher Education. (National Commission for Further and Higher Education, 2016:20)

Pressure is exerted on educational institutions to expand further their educational services. In countries where the public educational institutions cannot provide for such expansion, they are relying on privatized foreign educational institutions to meet such demand. An example of this is in Cyprus and Malta with increasing number of private institutions opening shop in both countries (Borg and Mayo, 2008). In Malta, morning and evening courses are provided by recognized UK universities including the universities of Leicester, London and Sheffield.

Despite the gap between those who have opportunities for tertiary education and those who don't, it is undoubtedly a fact that there has been a gradual increase in social mobility in the last few decades. A necessary precursor of this is in the rise in the number of students being the first generation of university graduates in their families (Halsey et al., 1980, Marshall et al., 1997, Reay, 2009). More young people are taking up courses before joining the workforce and are more likely to experience intergenerational mobility in light of the upsurge of graduates coming from working-class backgrounds – a tendency that defies Bourdieu and Wacquant (1992) notion of the process of habitus formation, as an enduring matrix of dispositions and as having a pivotal role in one's accumulation of resources. By referring to the British education system, Diane Reay (2009) looked at the rise in working-class children obtaining a degree and moving on to professional employment. In this case, such individuals are challenging the presumed unity of the habitus and instead they are developing a 'reflexive habitus' that traverses the dual fields they inhabit. They are prone to experience middle-class angst of being in an ambivalent class because of the difference in culture from their class of origin and their pressures to prove themselves in middle-class careers.

Education and social mobility

> As self-made men, they [the upwardly mobile] cannot have the familiar relation to culture which authorises the liberties and audacities of those who are linked to it by birth, that is, by nature and essence. (Bourdieu, 1984:331)

Studies associated with the works of Goldthorpe et al. (1969), including the work of Albert Henry Halsey (1980) and his colleagues at Nuffield College in Oxford, addressed the general attribution of intergenerational mobility since the Second World War. A key factor for the upward social mobility in post-war Britain was not only the transformative effects of the educational system, explored earlier on in this chapter, but also changes in the occupational structure through the growth in technical, managerial and professional occupations as well as the decline in blue-collar work in agriculture and manufacturing.

Within this field of study, various researches surrounding social mobility have been interested in quantitative analysis in the differences in educational attainment, by mediating the relationship between class of origin and destination education. It is worth sketching out studies on social mobility surrounding the notion of habitus and family background. For Bourdieu (1984), dispositions have their roots in one's habitus and stay unified through time; thus, those with strong initial reserves of cultural capital, acquired from the family, are bound to accumulate further capital through education and employment. On the other hand, those with low initial reserves would be prone to accumulate less resources. The constraints of social positioning, in this regard, appear the antithetical to the notion of social mobility.

Socially mobile individuals are said to have developed connections with different social groups through their cultural engagement and consumption patterns. The educational system gives them the tool kit to adapt to different cultural set of values associated with the middle class. They culturally adapt in social situations in the way they dress themselves, their choice in food and cultural participation. This is particularly true for well-educated socially mobile individuals in professional jobs, who want to fit in both with their class of origin and within their new social milieu. Unlike Thorstein Veblen's (1999 [1899]) analysis of the 'nouveau riche' in the United States and their efforts to exclude others who did not belong to their leisure class, the 'democratization' of conspicuous consumption focuses on inclusion (McGuigan, 2009).

There has been a notable shift in the way people are now exhibiting wide cultural taste, often translated into an inclination for a heterogeneity of cultural preferences of those who are habitually dubbed as 'cultural omnivores', primarily by Peterson and Simkus (1992). Additionally, the middle classes are said to be embracing and grazing on both 'high' and 'low' culture (Bennett et al., 2009). In a way, the omnivore theory refers to the tendency that socially mobile persons with tertiary education are more likely to embrace different cultural tastes. All these shifts are happening within the context of growing cultural industries since the second half of the twentieth century in tandem with a number of factors taking place such as the rising prosperity in the global North, rising literacy rates, the increase in leisure time and especially the accessibility of new technological media for communication.

The experience of being cultural omnivores has its advantages because persons with wide cultural tastes can find common denominator talk and develop strong social connections which transcend social class boundaries (Di Maggio, 1987). They feel at home in their culture of origin with their family and find a need to return ever so often. This was clearly apparent in the way tertiary-educated youth, who were socially mobile from their class of origin, still felt they had to return to their village for the annual *festa*, a popular folk religious feast (Visanich, 2015). Apart from omnivore predispositions, a recent study on *festa*-goers in Malta suggests that for a substantial group of persons occupying middle-class and professional jobs, reasons for active participation in the village *festa* go beyond omnivorness and has to do with their sense of belonging (Visanich, 2017). Their meanings and feelings on the *festa* and in particular their 'intimate engagement' with the patron saint, as a semi-idolatrous figure, are related to their nostalgic feelings of their class of origin. These meanings to this cultural events are underpinned by the degree of cohesion, family loyalty and communal outdoor summer celebrations, particularly typical in the South (Visanich, 2017).

Notwithstanding Bourdieu and Passeron's (1979) assertion on the way class inequalities are produced in the educational system limiting social mobility, recent studies refer to how the educational system is more than ever acting as a vehicle for upward social mobility. Yet it is noteworthy to consider that access to tertiary education, as a route to social mobility, often comes at a hefty cost.

As much as tertiary education is a painstaking process, it is equally a painful one – financially disabling youth from acquiring independence. This comes at a high cost, especially in light of the recent increase in tuition fees in various countries in Europe. Chapter 2 deals with this in more detail with reference to the increased costs in obtaining a degree.

> Young people face a dilemma. If they go to university they incur debts of over £50,000 and will be paying back their loans well into middle age. And in a number of cases they end up with degrees that don't get them into graduate jobs. (Lampl as interviewed by Adams, the Guardian online, 2018)

These are the concerns of Sir Peter Lampl, founder of the Sutton Trust charity for the promotion of social mobility through education in Britain.

These are also the concerns of millennials in tertiary education who aspire to enter the labour market effortlessly after graduation.

The next chapter builds on intergenerational social mobility, as one of the outcomes, not only of the expansion of the educational system but also due to increased academic credentials. It also explores the financial implications of entering into tertiary education in relation to other financial encumbrances encountered by millennials, principally when living within a culture of conspicuous consumption. This is fuelled by marketing mechanisms, often resulting in youth experiencing financial hardship before entering adulthood. This is explained in more detail in what follows.

2

The currency of academic credentials, consumerism and financial burdens

With the recent preposterous increase in tuition cost, university students in Britain blanch at the thought of having to pay tripling fees. 'A luxury that can only be afforded by those who are rich enough' declared in an affirmed voice a university student when speaking about the educational system, while marching to protest in London, with other dissed millennials against such measures in 2010 (Jones, 2010). Waving anarchist flags from the roof of the building housing the Conservative party headquarters, millennials in Westminster rallied against university funding cuts and demanded fair access to education. They voiced their distrust in governance tactic, based on neoliberal austerity measures. Matt Myers (2017) documented this in *Student Revolt: Voices of the Austerity Generation* by presenting oral histories of youth activists who took to the streets when tuition fees became unaffordable.

This chapter builds on this by unpacking the financial situation of millennials today, in part due to the real cost of pursuing post-compulsory education. It also builds on the previous chapter on the extension of educational systems and the increased weight put on obtaining qualifications to improve one's market situation. This is apparent in the rising numbers of young people earning a degree before entering into full-time work.

This chapter specifically focuses on academic capitalism in relation to the degree of 'credentialism' – a term used to refer to the reduction of qualifications, away from the meaning of enhancing the human potential, to the status of a certificate. Learning becomes a utilitarian task, with a constant relentless dilemma for students on whether they are getting their money's worth. Within the current climate of academic capitalism, universities are regarded as factories feeding the fundamental value of credentials in the workplace and acting as a kind of McUniversities, if you like, with mass-producing knowledge in hurried digestible bytes.

This chapter also explicitly focuses on the financial implications of extending years in education, with the consequence of entering into substantial debts before joining the workforce. This debt climate that is fuelled further by the surge in consumerist behaviour is addressed in this chapter for its considerable repercussions on the life experiences of millennials today. Albeit the harsh reality of rising costs of living, higher education and housing as well as the undermining of employment rights and pensions, youth are more than ever being seduced by corporations to have an affluent lifestyle. Everyday life experiences of youth are more than ever commodified. This has a significant impact on the 'cool' identity-formation and patterns in cultural consumption, having marketing mechanisms the main drivers of consumer seduction. This is examined in more detail in this chapter by referring to discourses on the structure–agency relations in consumerism amongst youth and their acts of resistance through subcultural activity.

Academic capitalism

There is rich literature on the economics of human capital investment. Education is considered as a pure investment to maximize high investment-returns, often measured by the currency of future earnings. In contemporary society, the occupational value of an individual's education is associated with the achievement of an educational title – this is the core of the sociological theory of educational credentials (Collins, 1979). As discussed in the works of Buchinsky and Leslie (2010) and that of Attanasio and Kaufmann (2012), the role of one's expectations of the labour market is treated as the direct outcome of schooling decisions.

Prioritizing efficiency, calculability, predictability and increased control with measureable processes in higher education is a new drive towards the corporatization practices of university administrators. The application of Ritzer's (1993) concept of McDonaldization, a popular and arguably emotive notion of new Taylorism for higher education, is applied to describe the transformations of universities, from knowledge generators to rational service organizations (Nadolny and Ryan, 2015).

What is called 'McUniversities' stands for nothing short of a factory of mass-producing knowledge. The McDonaldization in higher education implies increased similarities between work practices of universities and fast food restaurants: reliance on flexible labour, emphasizing quality rule and regulations and in some cases also franchising brand names of universities. In Ritzer's words, the McDonaldization process is

> an ever more instrumentally rationalised labour process mirrored in an equally instrumentalised sphere of consumer "choices" essentially already made, so that standardisation and efficiency become the unifying functional paradigm for society. (Ritzer,1993:9)

The increased globalization of universities, driven by innovation in information and communication technologies, as well as the growth in the internationalization of students, is what is given the perception that universities are mimicking corporations in their orientations (Healey, 2008). Within a neoliberal climate on increased drive to corporatization, universities are transforming themselves into markets, aiming to produce standardized knowledge (Parker, 2012).

However, it may be too naïve to assume a straightforward parallel of the two, without scrutinizing the complexities of the differences between them. It is essential to acknowledge the purpose and motives of fast food restaurants to generate profit by producing homogenous fast food. This is opposed to those of universities, whose goals are the acquisition and dissemination of knowledge (Nadolny and Ryan, 2015). Correspondingly, when universities attempt to mimic the market itself by managing its structures in standardize measures, it is in the process inadvertently building cumbersome and expensive bureaucracies (Lorenz, 2012) – this is in itself an antithesis of efficiency, one of the hallmarks of McDonaldization.

However, what is certain is that just like the operation of business industries, higher education is globalizing. Universities are more than ever an export sector, with licences to form franchising degrees with international partners of many of Europe's distinguished seats of learning. Franchising involves a university to sub-contract a local provider in another country to offer a degree programme under its brand name. Following the so-called 'Uppsala internationalization model', the sequencing of the internationalization of businesses follows four steps: first it is exporting, second licensing production, third joint ventures and fourth sole ventures (Johanson and Wiedersheim-Paul, 1975, Johanson and Vahlne, 1977).

It is not only universities that are turning global but also students – a large number of students, 1.6 million to be exact, were temporarily abroad for the purpose of undertaking tertiary-level studies across the EU in 2016, with more than two-fifths of these students (42.6 per cent) were from Europe, 29.7 per cent from Asia and 12.2 per cent from Africa (Eurostat, 2018b).

In this regard, financial support is crucial to facilitate student mobility. The average public expenditure on tertiary education, relative to gross domestic product, is 1.3 per cent in the EU28. This takes into consideration the direct expenditure on educational institutions, the support to students with scholarships and public loans, as well as transferring public subsidies for educational activities. In southern European countries, the percentage of public expenditure varies significantly, with Malta (1.4 per cent) having the largest rate, to Cyprus (1.1 per cent), Portugal (0.9 per cent), Italy (0.7 per cent) and Spain (0.95 per cent) (Eurostat, 2017).

Notwithstanding efforts for public subsidization in education and the vast possibilities for students' scholarships, especially in EU countries for youth to complete their tertiary education abroad, it is a reality that the majority of these youth end up taking students' loans with the consequence of having substantial debts before entering the workforce – for this reason, they were labelled as the 'Debt Generation' by Anya Kamenetz (2007).

The debt generation

On current trends, given the debt in university tuition fees, high rents and low wages, millennials are more prone to live in poverty compared to their predecessors. In 2017, around 28 per cent or 21.8 million of young Europeans aged between sixteen and twenty-nine were at risk of poverty or social exclusion in the EU, with women at slightly higher risk compared to men (Eurostat, 2018a). The highest levels of having young people at risk of poverty or social exclusion were in Greece (45.9 per cent) and Bulgaria (41 per cent) with the lowest rates being found in Slovakia (17.3 per cent) and Malta (15.3 per cent) (Eurostat, 2018a). Worryingly, this rate is also on the increase. The share of young people at risk of poverty in the EU is 2.9 per cent higher in 2017 compared to that of 2007.

Young households in countries like Belgium, Germany, Austria, the UK and to a lesser extent France, Italy and Malta are living worse off than their older counterparts (Eurostat, 2009). Less than 10 per cent of young households in Mediterranean countries like Italy, Spain, France, Cyprus and Malta maintain that they could not afford to buy a car, let alone a home. They are habitually priced out of home ownership and made to live a nomadic lifestyle of short-term rent contracts. Whereas consumption preferences vary according to different age-cohorts, in the 'Youth in Europe, A Statistics Portrait' survey (Eurostat, 2009), respondents were asked on their ability to purchase regardless of whether or not they actually wanted the item. For instance, young people had stronger preferences for computers and holidays away from home when compared to their older counterparts. This is evident in a relatively high share of European youth who form part of the tourist population. Nevertheless, whereas young people in countries like the Netherlands, Denmark, Luxemburg, Slovenia, Iceland and Norway maintained that more than 80 per cent of young households were able to afford a holiday, in countries like Malta and Portugal, more than 50 per cent of youth state that they could not afford such an expense (Eurostat, 2009). The need for young people to travel to other countries is not simply to satisfy the sense of adventure but, in more ways than one, it is a source of knowledge and personal development.

This ties in with a broader context of financial inequality. Unlike Beck's (1992) argument on 'ties to a social class recede mysteriously into the background [...] Status-based social milieus and lifestyles typical of a class culture lose their lustre' (1992:88), class polarization and inequality in the distribution of wealth are still very much part of the everyday life today. Whereas for some the concept of class has been pronounced as dead (Pakulski and Waters, 1996), for others it has been undergoing a renaissance in the new global context, with new inequalities growing worldwide (Klein, 2005 [2000]). This gap between the rich and the poor is visible everywhere and is increasing especially between

First World countries and Third World countries. Whereas consumer choice increased, it is too naïve to speak about consumer sovereignty, mainly because it is only a minority who are granted choices in society.

Naomi Klein (2005 [2000]) in *No Logo* articulated on how the gulf between the rich and poor countries is becoming widened by neoliberal globalization. The rapid diffusion of the revival of free-market economic policy had tremendous consequences both on a macro- and micro-level. One such consequence is the increase in transnational practices of companies, shifting production to cheap labour locations. The American journalist Anya Klein (2005 [2000]), in her ethnographic work, referred to the way brand-name multinational corporations produce their goods in free-trade zone for cheap labour and simply insist that they are just bargain hunters searching for best deals in the 'global mall'. The increasing desire for people to consume and the increase in transnational practices have resulted in deeper class polarization between the rich and the poor.

On an individual level, Kamenetz (2007) explored in detail the financial burden of young people. Although she focused specifically within the American social reality, this work can be seen as having wider applicability mainly in countries with continuous rising in tuition fees. Kamenetz (2007) exhausted her book *Generation Debt* with everyday accounts of young people to illustrate the crisis they are living through as a consequence of the current political climate. Primarily she highlighted the unequal distribution of economic resources in which older people are 'taking far more than their fair share' (2007:xiii).

The increase in tuition fees today contrasts sharply with the availability of grants during the post-Second World War years, as part of the expansion of public higher education. Notwithstanding that 'financial aid' is provided today to American students, the offered grants are a far cry from the remaining balance that needs to be settled by the student. As in the narrative account of one student 'Fred', Kamenetz (2007) wanted to stress the frustrating situation of students who anxiously wanted to obtain higher education yet lacked financial backing to do so – 'I registered for classes, showed up, and I wouldn't be on the roll. They drop you from classes if the cheque doesn't come. So I would crash classes to try to get in' (Kamenetz, 2007:28). Indeed, such desperate situations, partly the result of minimum state intervention, compel young people to give up on higher education with the hope of finding full-time employment. Student loans to finance higher education coupled with the culture of hedonistic consumerism, credit card debt and high cost of housing are resulting in a gloomy life situation for young people, not just in America but worldwide (Kamenetz, 2007). To add more to this equation of debt, millennials are synonymous to be more than ever immersed in the consumer culture due to their training into conspicuous consumption. This warrants a deep investigation into how consumer seduction operates to understand the dire financial situation of youth.

The origins of consumer seduction for youth

Young people in their twenties have grown up terribly absorbed in aggressive advertising. First, it should be pointed out that consumption is not simply a pleasurable affair – it has to do with the degree of affect associated with a novel product, the sense of excitement and delight in the feeling of strangeness and unfamiliarity of acquiring a new product (Williams, 2001). Thus, the experience of consumption is an affective one, played out, literally and metaphorically, in the insatiable quest to consume and the desire for endless longing for the new. The notion affect is seldom defined clearly. Some scholars ground their understanding of it in Deleuzian theories and treat affect as force and an intensity (Massumi, 2002).

Given the fleeting nature of desire, individuals are therefore on a constant search for acquiring a new commodity or experience. Experiences in consumption constitute a kind of rational hedonism and pleasure seeking, involved in a series of imaginative scenarios based on fantasy, desire and day-dreaming. Through the language of advertising, commodities are made to entice us in various ways, not only in their aesthetic appeal and sensual qualities but also in the status or prestige associated with the labelling of the product and the fantasies that are imbued by consumers.

It bears much truth to say that youth in the late modernity are amongst the fiercest segment of the population to be seduced by this form of commodity fetishism. Yet it is incorrect to assume that such commodity fetishism amongst youth is a contemporary phenomenon. It has been argued that the popularization of consumption had a direct impact on the making of 'teenager' as an independent life stage which became particularly associated with consumption patterns after the Second World War. Jon Savage (2008) in his work *Teenage* explored this stage as a time of 'living in the now, pleasure seeking, product-hungry, embodying the new global society where social inclusion was to be granted through purchasing power ... The future would be teenage' (Savage, 2008:465). In the comparatively affluent Anglo-American post-war years, the teenage years, between the ages of thirteen to nineteen, became a distinct social and economic life stage, peddled by marketing mechanisms and expressed through the consumption of products such as magazines and clothes.

The basic rule for marketing, according to Alissa Quart (2003) in her book *Branded: The Buying and Selling of Teenagers*, is to 'get 'em while they're young' (2003:9). Quart considered youth as the worst-hit victims of conspicuous consumption mainly because they were immersed into embracing the logic of consumerism from an early age with branded toys. The trend of viral marketing, or peer-to-peer marketing, is adopted to spread the seductive lure of brands and infiltrate the minds and hearts of the young. Young girls are recruited to attend brand focus groups to offer their 'consultation' to marketers on what is hip. These girls admitted that consulting was a way of defending oneself from bullying at school and ensuring a place amongst the so-called 'cool' gang. Quart (2003) explored the semiotics attached with brands in her conversation with these girls who wear designer label clothes, often associated with women twice their age. These girls, parading in shopping malls, driven by deep desires for beauty, have a fixation on purchasing clothes and perfumes. Shopping malls create an ambiguous and anxious environment of needing, which is only released by buying. In one of the conversations Quart (2003) had with the girls and their mothers, it is clear how these girls want to look like affluent adults, wearing the same brands like their parents and having a strong desire to transform their child-like body into a sexy one. They are regarded by Quart (2003) as passively accepting conspicuous consumption from a very young age and brought up in a society which values appearance above all else. Dubbed as 'influencers', some parents, children and young people are now resorting to social media, blogs and vlogs to reach the same objective to popularize toys, trends and 'cool' devices, rather than parading in shopping malls.

Conspicuous consumption, marketing seduction and subcultural identities

Discourse on conspicuous consumerism is habitually surrounded on the relation between structure and agency – despite being generally regarded as antithetical. It makes sense to explore the connection between them to frame discourse on identity formation of young adults through consumption. Thus, herein I look at the way young people are seen as gullible consumers, an approach highly inspired by the Frankfurt school, and analyse studies that deal with personal agency when using consumer goods, inspired by the works of Paul Willis (1990) and his likes on subcultures.

The structured approach of the Frankfurt school is about the pervasive implication of consumption as a tool for the ideology sustained by the capitalists and used to reinforce mechanisms of social control. From this viewpoint, market segments are simply regarded as tailored to capture everyone within the web of consumption – an ideology mirroring the Marxists ideas of Theodor Adorno and Max Horkheimer (1997) on the controlling forces of the culture industry. Ever since market segmentation replaced the old Taylorist theory of the 1960s, individuals feel that they have more choice to consumers' products which give them a distinctive identity. This element of diversity in consumer goods is seen as simply an illusion serving the function for the provision of all 'so none may escape' (Adorno and Horkheimer, 1997:123). Their study has been written with conviction that the role of the media is to send uniform messages to the masses that work to retain the class gap through the culture industry by encouraging false sense of hope for the working class. They maintained that

> the culture industry perpetually cheats its consumers of what it perpetually promises ... The promise, which is actually all the spectacle consists of, is illusory: all it actually confirms is that the real point will never be reaches that the diner must be satisfies with the menu. (Adorno and Horkheimer, 1997:139)

What is referred to as 'the culture ideology of consumerism' by Leslie Sklair (2002) is an intrinsic part of the contemporary economic globalization in which the capitalist system is generated by reinforcing a system of market dependency. This system perpetuates the accumulation of capital for private profit and, in other words, ensures the continuation of the capitalist global system (Sklair, 2002). This has implications particularly on youth as a generation, who have more than ever a global exposure to the same commodities in popular culture. McCrindle and Wolfinger (2010) went as far as to suggest that we are witnessing, for the first time, a 'global generation' due to popular culture and global consumption – 'a generation accessing the same websites, watching the same movies, downloading the same songs and being influenced by the same brands' (2010:2). Such patterns in global consumption are having substantial implications on the changing meaning of leisure within the postmodern society. In line with Chris Rojek's (1995) observations, in his book *Decentring Leisure,* leisure is not only related to the idea of freedom but it has become more diverse than simply an 'escape' from everyday life. He sustained that leisure should not be seen as a separate aspect of social life but as part of other experiences and within its social context. In addressing the shift in leisure activities from modern to postmodern societies, he argued that with the use of simulations and virtual reality machines, leisure in postmodernity has lost its distinctiveness as an activity away from work. Leisure has become an end in itself instead of an activity designed to reach a goal or to pursue an authentic experience. This is particularly the case when examining how global transnational communication companies are 'packaging' experiences, for instance, and in the process blurring the distinction between work and leisure.

Living in the 'Age of Access', an era governed by a new set of market work ethics, the focus is on the marketing and selling of cultural experiences rather than just based on the traditional industrial-based goods and services (Rifkin, 2000). Within this new era of cultural hypercapitalism, in global travel and tourism as well as within the industries of entertainment, wellness, fashion, sports and media companies, more weight than ever is put on the marketing of access to new experiences. This global 'experience' economy often mine local cultural resources of different locations, repackage and sell them as cultural commodities and entertainment (Rifkin, 2000). Specifically peddled by transnational media companies, manufactured goods and basic services promote cultural experiences.

It is undeniably the fact that in recent years, mobile technological portable devices are amongst the most fetishized commodities by millennials who lived through the popularization and accessibility of these devices during their coming of age. 'To those who say they've seen it all, I say, buckle your seatbelt, the future is about to begin' (Gibbs, online, 2019), affirmed DJ Koh, the head of Samsung's mobile business as he held the new Samsung phone Galaxy Fold aloft. These devices are often advertised for their degree of empowerment, ease in use and connectivity to your peers and to the world in a form of a 'windowed shell' allowing mobile privatization of the individualized user wherever you are. Such devices play a significant role in the transmission of flows of information on a global platform. The media presents what Baudrillard (1988) called 'the ecstasy of communication' through the production of endless procession of cultural fragments creating euphoria for the viewers. It is made to excite viewers and form simulated fantasies in the process of creating simulated lived experiences especially for young people.

Manuel Castells (1996, 1997, 1998) strikes a typical note in his three-volume series *The Information Age: Economy, Society and Culture* on the changes in the role of Information and Communication Technologies (ICTs). He claimed that the dynamics of the information age rests on three pillars: the technological revolution, the reconstruction of capitalism and statism, and the emergence of social cultural movements. However, throughout his study, he emphasized mostly the importance of technological innovation to an extent that he was criticized of technological determinism. He suggested that changes in social relations are instigated by technological changes.

However apart from their essential function of connectivity, portable devices are also used as markers of distinction and status. Obtaining a 'cool' identity is hallmark especially for millennials. Consumption is a tool within the 'cool capitalism' (McGuigan, 2009) to present a self that says a lot about one's cultural tastes, one's awareness on what's hip and possibly one's social positioning. Some 'cool' products are marketed as offering individuality through their distinctive characteristics and functions.

This ties in to the fact that the market is no longer driven by mass production but by market segmentation, targeting and creating the needs and desires of different target groups. Whether it is the new Jaguar advert promoting a 'breed apart' for those who want to feel exclusive and privileged, or the Nike shoes advert, promoting wide range of identities, from the 'artistic' to the 'caution' collection, commodities are marketed with in-built identity symbols. Such distinctions are examples of the ways how marketing mechanisms peddle the idea that consumer goods enable groups to include whilst excluding others. Herein Pierre Bourdieu's (1984 [1979]) work on distinction is useful to refer to differences in tastes. However, recent studies also show how discourse on taste distinction in relation to class is now highly contested. The notion of cultural capital, as a conceptual tool for accentuating privilege by the dominant social classes, is highly questioned in this regard and viewed as reductive and deterministic.

The use of commodities: agency and subcultural capital

The critical view on market dependency of youth often suggests a passive generation gullible of everything the market throws at them. The sense of youths' agency is apparent in the way millennials are not stoically experiencing the uncertainties of their situations without reacting.

In spite of the negative stereotypes abound on millennials, Neil Howe and William Strauss (2000) sustained that this generation is poised to become the 'next great generation', for they are more group-oriented and have a working ethos to change things, including in their rebellion against political cynicisms and social ennui, compared to previous generations. Despite this generic vision of this generation, there are hints of truth in Howe and Strauss's arguments. It is undeniably the case that millennials are poignantly reacting to the neoliberal socio-economic situation they are living through and ostensibly striving for change. It is not surprising than that the word *youthquake* was chosen as the Oxford Dictionaries word of the year in 2017. To put it succinctly, this refers to the recent cultural, political or social change as a consequence of actions or influence of young people and their reflexive awareness of youth striving for change. Students are now increasingly organizing themselves through coordinating over their mobile phones and social networking sites. They are also becoming more environmentally conscious, anti-capitalists and opting for alternative greener fair-trade goods. The so-called hipters or bohos youths are usually very much driven by displaying semiotics that are read out as unconventional. The labour conditions in the production of branded gear are often exposed to raise awareness on the system of exploitation.

The rather recent phenomenon of 'culture jamming' by anti-capitalist movement activists is one example of the empowerment of people to do something about the pervasive effect of corporations. In a form of 'semiotic Robin Hoodism', cultural jamming referred to adbusters and their mission is of 'hijacking billboards in order to drastically alter their messages' (Klein, 2000:280). Recent youth movements, whether political, New Age travellers, eco-warriors and anti-capitalist movements are not just pleasure-seeking individuals but they do show strong elements of subcultural characteristics including in their verve for resistance (Blackman, 2005).

Nonetheless, this notion of agency in consumption and general dispositions is not a new phenomenon. Since the late 1990s, the idea of youth as cultural dupes has been highly disputed in studies on youth subcultures who explored the confines of class or structuralist analysis and how youth actively choose alternative use of consumption in identity formation.

An example of this approach is Paul Willis's work on *Common Culture* (1990) in his examination of how young people consume actively in creative ways, transforming the original meaning of the commodity to create a personal identity in a process of symbolic exchange. Rather than being simply consumers, millennials are prosumers in the way they produce the products they consume. The role of producers and consumers is more than ever blurred with the rise in mass customization of products, since the time Alvin Toffler (1980) coined the term 'prosumers' forty years ago. Millennials encode the commodity with their own set of meanings, thus refashioning it creatively. The use of music, as a critical feature for identity construction, is an exemplary case of this negotiation process between the actual product of the music industry and how it intertwines with individual biography and location (Bennett, 2000:195):

> On the one hand, music informs ways of being in particular social spaces; on the other hand, music functions as a resource whereby individuals are able to actively construct those spaces in which they live. Thus, in a real sense, music not only informs the construction of the self, but also the social world in which the self operates.

Another exemplary case of youths' agency in relation to consumption is in the way youth, during the post-war years, were actively challenging social and economic measures that resulted in an 'affluent' society through their subcultural activity. The term 'affluence' was highly contested for not always denoting positive connotations of an improved society but of a more consumerist one. The post-war economist JK Galbraith (1958), in his study *The Affluent Society*, saw this 'affluence' in America as being governed by false needs, contrived by advertising, in which people never had so many goods rather than never 'had it so good'. This increase in material production does not necessarily equate to a healthy American society. What's more, for Galbraith (1958), private affluence came at the expense of public squalor because of the lack of social and physical infrastructure within the public sector that was overshadowed by what was labelled as 'artificial affluence' by the production of commercial goods. This was one of the underlying factors in the intensification of 'artificially created desires' which had their roots during the 1960s in the 'golden age of capitalism' (Sklair, 2002:62).

Other scholars like Richard Hoggart (1958) in *The Uses of Literacy* also referred to the negative side effects of 'affluence' in Britain because it brought about cultural impoverishment and the loss of working-class values. In particular, shifts in the class structures with increased opportunities for social mobility inspired the creation of youth subcultures. This was aptly documented by British academics associated with the Birmingham Centre for Contemporary Cultural Studies of the 1970s (Hall and Jefferson,1976, Willis, 1978, Hebdige, 1979). Youth subcultures exemplify the way young people congregate together, due to their shared class position, to express their style and obtain a sense of belonging from the group. The understanding of identity of oneself and of others is an integral part of social life because it is only when people distinguish different identities that they can relate to each other (Jenkins, 1996). It involves establishing similarities and differences between social groups.

Speaking about this, Phil Cohen (1972) fittingly explained the development of working-class subcultures in their efforts to voice their dissatisfaction on the shifts in classes in the 1960s resulting in the increased availability of office jobs as opposed to working-class manual work. The skinheads were actively resisting and resenting the changes in the working class and the false air of hopes provided by social workers. They simply wanted a return to their working-class traditions by rebuilding the traditions of their parent working-class culture due to its assumed collective solidarity, its conception of masculinity and its orientation towards the 'outsiders'. Similar reactions to class relations were observed by Paul Willis (1978) when he studied the actions of motorbike subcultural boys who resisted the dominant culture because of their deprived material conditions. On the other hand, the mods, a group of working-class youth doing lower middle-class jobs, were also reacting to this shift by accentuating their upward class position through their dispositions, attire and adopting an Italianate *bellavita* lifestyle (Hebdige, 1976).

Subcultural studies often presented an overemphasis overview of youths' social action, what Kellner calls the 'fetishism of resistance' (1994:37). It is often the case that scholars 'positioned conceptually youth culture and youth subculture in a relation of resistance, to, or, rebellion towards a dominant culture' (Redhead, 1990:41). Jim McGuigan (1992) stated that the 'working class subcultures of "resistance" – teds, mods, rockers, skins, punks and so on – were read politically as symbolic challenges to the dominant culture' (1992:89–90). An exemplary was the Punk subculture in the 1970s which epitomized such resistance by reacting to the economic climate at that time, with high rates of youth unemployment. Their rebellion personas reflected the 'gloomy apocalyptic ambience of the late 1970s' (Hebdige:122–123) characterized by instability as a consequence of crisis of organized capitalism and the right political turn to the neoliberal ideology.

However, such resistance was adapted in relation to the socio-economic and cultural conditions of different locations. Take the punk scene in Portugal for instance which can be used as an exemplary case in the way youth in the South used their own strategies of negotiation and accommodation to what was happening elsewhere in relation to their 'delayed' economic shifts (Guerra, 2018). As opposed to countries in the Anglo-American context, Portuguese society, similar to other southern European countries with 'slow-motion' cultural changes, witnessed the emergence of style-based youth culture during the 1980s and 1990s. This was due to the fact that Portugal's post-revolutionary context and its integration into the European Community in 1986 played an important role in legitimizing different youth's lifestyles. Other important changes, permitting cultural changes in Portugal and other countries in the south, were the liberalization of national television, the introduction of cable television and the popularization of satellite television in the 1990s. Because of political dictatorship in Portugal, young people were restricted to follow through the routes to subcultural activity. Nonetheless, punk subculture still found ways to grow through DIY practices, including through sewing their own clothes due to lack of ready-made clothes available before the 1980s. It was not only in clothes, but the DIY culture was adopted when it came to doing Mohican hairstyles, tattoos and body piercings (Guerra, 2018).

It is worth addressing that debates on the conceptualization of youth (sub) cultures are polarized – those supporting the subcultural theory as derived from the Centre for Contemporary Cultural Studies (CCCS) on the use of the same semiotics, dress code and listening to the same music as a distinguishable feature of subculture identity as opposed to those who support a more individualized understanding. Subcultural theory has been criticized for excluding commonalities between different social groups. Andy Bennett, in particular, reframed the concept of collective youth identities using Maffesoli's concept of neo-tribes (Bennett, 2005). Michel Maffesoli (1996) does not agree that we are experiencing the end of collective identities. In contrast, the increase in communalized or collectivized empathy, based on multiple forms of 'being together', gives rise to a form of neo-tribalism. This less structured system of 'neo-tribes', within hybrid cultures, is what is now favourably considered to describe the recent fluid groupings of people with similar interests. Postmodernists stressed on the way personal identity is much more fluid, less structured and based on pick-and-mix free-floating choices through consumption. The overemphasis is on diversity and the lack of rules and boundaries of youth cultural activity.

Cashing on counter-culture identities

It is an undeniable fact that young people who actively were part of a subculture were not simply always passive recipients of the market but reflectively creating their own styles as a sign of resistance. Yet, the market still plays a central part in these counter-culture groups by slowly commercializing such signs of resistance. The ideas on creating counter-culture identities build in with what Sarah Thornton (1996) has said on the temporary phase of 'subcultural capital'. Briefly put, subcultural capital became a momentary phase enjoyed by a minority until it reaches mainstream and loses its significance.

Derived from Bourdieu's cultural capital, subcultural capital denotes control over those who do not possess it. Subcultural capital is the 'marker of hipness and being in the know' (Thornton, 1996:10) – although it is only a transitional and temporary phase. It is the stage when the subcultural characterization is limited only to the minority. This stage is preceded by the internalization of these characteristics in popular culture. New counter-cultural trends and stylistic appearance, initially adopted by the minority cultural group, are becoming popularized for their distinctiveness as part of the marketing strategy. The media play a determinant role in the creation and destruction of subcultures. Thornton stated that

> while subcultural studies have tended to argue that youth subcultures are subversive until the very moment they are represented by the mass media, here it is argued that these kinds of taste cultures become politically relevant only when they are framed as such. In other words derogatory media coverage is not the verdict but the essence of their resistance. (Thornton, 1996:137)

Counter-cultural identities are losing their initial distinctiveness upon reaching popularization; 'the problem of underground subcultures is a popularization by a gushing up to the mainstream' (Thornton, 1996:5). This is being done through various ways. Negative coverage in the media, for example, automatically promotes subcultural capital for its distinctiveness and sows the seeds for its destruction upon gaining a popularized status. Thus, approval by the media is the kiss of death for a subculture.

This idea is in consistent with the comments made by Angela McRobbie (1994) on discourses of moral panic in the media and public spaces. Youth are often represented in a romanticized manner as a problematic group, especially in subcultural studies of the 1970s. The media and commercial marketing mechanisms are absorbing the former rebellious youth subcultural styles, giving them a populist 'cool' edge and selling them as commodities (Hebdige, 1988). Agencies of signification such as television are incorporating such styles into the mainstream. McRobbie (2005) elaborated on this form of moral panic in relation to the 'hoodie' culture in Britain and the way it provoked anxiety at its initial stages. McRobbie indicated the origin of this contemporary youth fashion expression from the black American hip-hop culture. The 'hoodie' culture is now considered part of mainstream popular culture due to the global economy of music through rap pop idols. The Rap music culture denotes insolence and rebellious behaviour in relation to social exclusion and signifies anger and rage. However, the autonomy of clothing in public spaces is being challenged in Britain with the prohibition of hooded tops obscuring the face in shopping centres. According to McRobbie (2005), the reaction to this prohibition results to further its popularity because it promotes this style as a representation of distinctiveness and anti-social behaviour. Another contemporary form of counter-cultural identity, which lost its distinctiveness and became popularized, is the 'Emo' culture. Emo, short for emotional hardcore punk rock, was a form of underground music in the late 1980s. It describes emotional performances of bands singing poetic, ecstatic songs with an inner meaning of break the limitations of the self.

This argument of youths' agency and their resistance to consumerism has been called into question more than twenty years ago by Thomas Frank (1997) in the *Conquest of Cool*. He stressed that capitalism is dynamic in its nature rather than static. This is evident in the dramatic changes in the way corporations were organized during the last fifty years.

The introduction of 'market segmentation' in the 1960s and the discovery of demographics replaced the manufacturing of one uniform product for everyone. Advertisements in the 1960s gave the impression that the consumer culture was a fraud while portraying consumers as individuals, standing out of a crowd rather than fitting in. Writing in consistent with this argument, Judith Williamson (1978), in *Decoding Advertisements*, maintained that advertisements are made to incorporate critique as a marketing strategy; 'ads which can incorporate criticisms of themselves have a much higher credibility than those which don't' (Williamson, 1978:174). Whereas American capitalism in the late 1950s dealt more with conformity and 'keeping up with the Joneses', the 1960s based their marketing strategies 'on the doctrine of liberation and continual transgression that is still familiar today' (Frank, 1997:20).

Instead of the physical characteristics of the product, market segmentation and consumer identity became prominent in modern theories of marketing (Frank, 1997). By the 1960s, idealized vision of American life captured in advertising seemed unbelievable and the 'creative revolution' with its carnivalesque characteristics and its embracing to the critique of mass society quickly replaced the ads of the 1950s (Frank, 1997). Robin Murray (1988), speaking about the Post-Fordist age, maintained that 'innovation has become a leading edge of the new competition... designers produce the innovation ... they shape lifestyles ... they are the engineers of designer capitalism' (Murray, 1988:166).

The welcoming of youth-led revolution and the meaning of hip, as a set of liberating practices at odds with the dominant impulses of post-war American society, were perceived by the American marketers as something that revitalizes the youth market rather than an act to bring down capitalism. Anchored within a specific social and economic context, the concepts of conformity and collectivism in contrast to individualist ethic are the by-products of shifts in the economy coupled by state manoeuvres and private corporations. They are the protagonists that swerve mass society into different so-called 'characterological' type in relation to the transformations in the economy, whether in times of economic stability or crisis (Frank, 1997). Of course, this sociological reasoning makes more sense when examining the dispositions of different youth generations existing at different historical moments and living through different socio-economic and cultural climates.

Frank (1997) argued that symbolic contestations were easily becoming incorporated into mainstream culture and simply became another market segment. Especially, but not exclusively, for the younger generation, market researchers break down the market both vertically by class and status and horizontally by group identities, age, gender and region or ethnicity in an attempt to seduce consumers with products designed for their 'needs'. Some 'cool' products are marketed as offering individuality through their distinctive characteristics and functions.

Frank (1997) examined the roots of counter-culture by analysing 'the forces and logic that made rebel youth cultures so attractive to corporate decision-makers' (Frank, 1997:7). By tracing the roots of bohemian cultural style, he argued that counter-culture rather than being the product of youth's dissatisfaction with capitalism is more the brainchild of lascivious businesses trying to sell unconventionality. In effect, he preferred to use the term 'fake' counter-culture in his 'co-optation' theory:

> Faith in the revolutionary potential of 'authentic' counterculture combines with the notion that business mimics and mass-produces fake counterculture in order to cash in on a particular demographic and to subvert the great threat that "real" counterculture represents. [In a nutshell] if you can't beat 'em, absorb 'em. (Frank,1997:7)

By referring to catalogue ads and commercials, Frank (1997) demonstrated the normality of this imagery of fake counter-culture in the 1960s. He maintained that it is very hard to distinguish between 'authentic' counter-culture and a fake one. He went on to argue that even the authenticity of counter-culture divorced from capitalism is somewhat difficult to find because most 'authentic' counter-cultures have their grassroots in mass culture. Its major protagonists are usually rock stars or millionaire performers and employees of the culture industry, and thus there is close affiliation with the capitalist consumer world. In spite of the claims made by subcultural scholars on youth's resistance of the dominant culture, teenage subcultures in post-war years are appropriately seen by Frank (1997) as the product of market capitalism. In line with this, hippies are regarded by Warren Hinckle (1967) as an integral part of the consumer culture.

> In the commercial sense, the hippies have not only accepted assimilation …, they have swallowed it whole. The hippie culture is in many ways a prototype of the most ephemeral aspect of the larger American society; if the people looking in front the subsurbs want change, clothes, fun and some lightheadedness form the new gypsies, the hippies are delivering – and some of them are becoming rich hippies because of it. (Hinckle, 1967:226)

Conclusion

This chapter dealt with the financial constraints of millennials, not only in relation to increased tuition fees that tie them to repayment schedules way into their adulthood, but also in terms of the cultural of conspicuous consumption and the quest for identity formation and subcultural activity. In an environment with increased credentialism, more pressure is put on one's market situation, performativity and employability. Young people are increasingly choosing to further their education with the consequence of entering into debts. This generation has also been trained into a conspicuous culture of consumption and seduced by 'artificially created desires' – an ideology which stresses the benefits of consumerism to satisfy artificially created desires which result in added financial burdens.

This chapter dealt with discourses on the structure–agency relation in consumerism amongst youth – on the one hand, how youth are looked at as cultural dupes with maxed out credit cards and financial repayment schedules; yet, on the other hand, they are also considered as active agents and prosumers in control of their situation. Herein, youth are assumed as active recipients, reflectively constructing their own distinctive subjectivities. Undeniably though, the dire financial situation is a reality in their everyday life especially since they are also at the frontline of precariat neoliberal economic conditions, experiencing high rate of casualization at work, unemployment and underemployment. This is discussed in more detail in the next chapter.

3

Unemployment in the graduate economy

Some of the reasons why millennials are living with pulse-pounding fretfulness are due to the permeating culture of uncertainty in the job market caused by the rising rates of youth unemployment. The global youth unemployment stood at 13 per cent in 2017, amounting to approximately 70.9 million unemployed youths (International Labour Organization, 2017). On a European level, 15.653 million men and women in the EU28 were unemployed in May 2019. The lowest rates of unemployment were observed in Germany, Czechia and the Netherlands, while the highest were recorded in the southern European countries of Greece, Italy and Spain (Eurostat, 2019d).

This chapter elaborates on how the workforce is evermore 'flexible', with a decline in a career-long mode of employment as opposed to the rise in contingent job contracts. This is observed with reference to its repercussion on the school to work transition; what was once a smooth transition from school to full-time employment for previous youth generations has become gradually potholed, lengthy and a multilinear process. The normalization of short-time contracts and having periods of unemployment is now part of millennials' biographical patterns. Neoliberal labour market forces obliterated the normality of a 'job for life' and brought about an increased disruption from the school to work transition. As a consequence, this brought about the blurring and even disintegration of life course divisions.

This chapter deals with examining further the school to work trajectories and the recent so-called 'patchwork careers' characterized by part-time and casual jobs interspersed with periods of unemployment. It explores how the workforce is much more flexible than ever before due to contingent contracts and mobile workforce. It also traces changes in the labour market, from the so-called 'affluence' of post-war period, based on social and economic measures to make sense of the changes in the standard of living of youth in the last sixty years. This chapter looks at austerity measures in southern European countries like Greece and Spain and their impact on the life experiences of youth. Principally, it makes sense of the high number of young people experiencing unemployment, forced migration and tendencies for depression as one of the consequences of such instability.

The common post-war Anglo-American experience

In the last two decades, various researches accentuated how the economic and political climate, coupled with the transformation of work, had contributed to an increasing ever fragmented school to work transition for youth compared to the experiences of their predecessors during the post-Second World War period (Heinz, 1991, Evans and Furlong, 1997, Mills and Blossfeld, 2001, Furlong and Cartmel, 2007[1997]). An understanding of this shift requires making sense of work opportunities for youth in the last six decades.

Post-war measures to trigger economic growth and consequentially improve the standard of living and working conditions of citizens have arguably paved the way to a smooth school to work transition (Ashton and Field, 1976). Writing about this assumed unilineal transition, Ashton and Field (1976) in *Youth Workers: The Transition from School to Work* addressed the predictable and uncomplicated nature of youths' life course transitions during that time. They identified different youth groups, each attaching diverse meaning to work and experience. For instance, the group they called 'the extended careers', associated with youth coming from middle-class backgrounds, were those who focused on long-term rewards through academic paths. Their long period in post-compulsory education guaranteed them high and secure incomes. This assurance was partly the outcome of social, political and economic changes within the Anglo-American context (Ashton and Field, 1976).

As for those youth who did not undergo any kind of training and joined the workforce at school-leaving age, they are said to have equally enjoyed prosperous opportunities; 'leaving school at the earliest opportunity and going straight into full-time work has the obvious advantage that a young person can become quickly financially independent' (Pollock, 1997:625). The low level of unemployment and high average weekly earnings provided a smooth move for youth into financial autonomy.

The pillars of the thriving economic environment as well as the power of trade unions at that time arguably strengthened and secured youth as an intermediary life course. Conventionally, young people were offered protection through institutionalized means whilst securing the homogenizing pathway leading to adulthood (Pollock, 1997).

Yet, was this transition really as smooth as assumed during this period? Despite the validity of the argument of Pollock and his likes, some scholars questioned the extent to which it was in fact as straightforward and smooth as presumed in the late 1950s and 1960s (Vickerstaff, 2003, Goodwin and O'Connor, 2005). Sarah Vickerstaff (2001), for instance, doubted this post-war smooth transition for those youth following apprenticeship. Rather than being a single straightforward step transition, she explained that their experiences were much more fragmented than anticipated. She admitted that choices available led to 'greater homogenization of possible pathways and individuals may have had less expectations of being able to design their own trail' (2001:3); however, she said that it was far from a straightforward transition. They still 'had to negotiate and manage their own trajectory, whether it was of their own choosing or not' (2001:3). In another study, John David Goodwin and Henrietta O'Connor (2005) expanded on the level of complexity that characterized youth's transition in the 1960s and 1970s. They focused on Leicester as their case study to contest the linearity of such transition. For them, the conventional wisdom of a smooth transition is underestimated as it ignored the degree of complexities experienced by youth at that time. Also, another important factor was that youths' transition to work was still very much gender-segregated. Young males were making 'mass transitions from the classroom to the factories and building sites, while young women followed pathways leading straight from school to shops, offices and factories' (Furlong and Cartmel, 2007[1997]:12).

Nonetheless, it is still safe to say that the youth generation entering the workforce in the early 1960s had a relatively smooth transition compared to millennials today. They benefitted directly from the Keynesian notion of full employment in places like Britain, which meant that there were more vacant jobs than available workers.

Measures for unemployment were safeguarded and enshrined in the 1945 Charter of the Universal Human Rights of United Nations. In the book *Full Employment in a Free Society*, Beveridge (1944) presented measures to maintain employment in a healthy society. He stressed that

> full productive employment in a free society is possible ... it is a goal that can be reached only by conscious continuous organisation of all our productive resources under democratic control. (Beveridge, 1944:16)

Further to his social security proposals in what is known as the *Beveridge Report*, Beveridge highlighted possibilities and strategies for achieving full employment by the state allowing citizens to have freedom in choosing their occupation and manage their personal income. Besides reducing unemployment to short intervals, Beveridge also proposed fair wages for jobs.

Security in society during this period was supported by what the economists Mitchell and Muysken (2008) in *Full Employment Abandoned* identified as the three main pillars of economic and social settlement. The first 'economic pillar' was based on the commitment to full employment which was achieved by the Keynesian fiscal and monetary demand management. This involved providing employment in the public sector and having the government mediating class struggle. Secondly, the 'redistributive pillar' was designed to improve market outcomes through state intervention that reduces the levels of unemployment. Underpinning the two pillars was the 'collective pillar' which provided various citizenship rights including comprehensive public health and educational systems to all citizens.

Because of low rates of unemployment, young people lived in times of prosperity and had much better benefits and opportunities than previous generations – they surely had 'far more independent spending power than their predecessors' (Hobsbawn, 1996:327).

Hobsbawn (1996) emphasized the benefits of this economic system for youth and the working population by arguing that

> an economy of mass consumption came into existence on the basis of full employment and regularly rising real incomes, buttressed by social security, which in time was paid for by rising public revenues. Indeed, in the euphoric 1960s some incautious governments went so far as to guarantee the unemployed – who were then few – 80 per cent of their former wage. (1996:282)

In view of this economic climate, The British Conservative politician Harold Macmillan won the general election in 1959 on the slogan that the post-war population 'never had it so good' (Black and Pemberton, 2004:2). Indeed, the socio-economic developments taking place during this time, till the early 1970s, resulted in affluent life chances especially for youth. Post-war British Labour and Conservative governments were committed to state intervention to maintain social cohesion – resulting in 'domestic peace and tranquillity, some sort of class compromise between capital and labour' (Harvey, 2005:10). Britain was not an exceptional case for such prosperous years. Similar actions in the United States were implemented to overcome the symptoms of the 'Great Depression' originated around 1929. In tandem with these measures, substantial advancement in technology brought significant developments in the United States and western European countries throughout the late 1950s and up to the late 1960s (Hobsbawn, 1996). This included technological advancement in the privatized lifestyles of individuals. Because of the increase in economic security, people were adjusting to a climate of increased economic security and the rising of material expectations. The higher standards of domestic comfort were enhanced with consumer durables and well-furnished homes. An economy of mass consumption came into existence due to the financial security of full-employment and regularly rising real incomes. During this prosperous period, some incautious governments went so far as to guarantee the unemployed, who were then few, 80 per cent of their former wage (Hobsbawn, 1996:282).

Changes in the labour market

The 'golden age' in employment opportunities did not survive beyond the 1960s. The 1970s were defined by crisis in capital accumulation, surging unemployment, inflation and 'stagflation' – a term coined by British politician Iain McIeod to refer to a situation with persistent high inflation, combined with high unemployment and stagnant growth in a country's economy (McKinnon, 2011). Economic growth driven by 'embedded liberalism' became exhausted and is 'no longer working' (Harvey, 2005:12). In such a dull economic climate, a group of economists inspired by Hayek and Friedman took advantage in implementing their economic plan for the liberation of corporate business power, the re-establishment of market freedom which brought about significant changes in the job market.

Various societal, economic and technological transformations were the drivers for the transformation of work, including changes in employment patterns, shifts in job conditions and an increase in precarious employment. In recent years, the dismantling of the Weberian 'iron cage' structure, made up of fixed corporate organization of bureaucracy, resulted in the ever-changing working conditions within the 'new economy' – what Richard Sennett (2006) referred to as the new form of 'flexible capitalism'. One definite aspect of this new system is the lack of long-term stability and benefits for the workers who have to face continuous uncertainties and risk without established guidelines.

Work is increasingly disorganized because nothing is 'fixed, given and certain, while everything rests upon much greater knowledge and information' (Lash and Urry, 1994:10–11). The notion of 'flexible capitalism', with its intensified flexible commoditization, refers to the kind of structural changes in the work environment. Workers are asked to behave nimbly, to be open to changes on short notice, to take risks continually and to become even less dependent on regulations and formal procedures. For Richard Sennett, three major phenomena stem from this form of institutionalization of flexible capitalism.

Firstly, due to high level of geographical mobility partly because of short-term job contracts, there has been the breakdown in attachment to place. In the last decade, the rate of temporary employees as a percentage of the total number of employees in most European countries had increased (European Commission, 2018). The number of European workers employed on fixed-term contracts for the EU average was 10.7 per cent in 2005 and had increased to 11.3 per cent in 2017, with the highest rates in southern European countries such as Spain (22.1 per cent), Portugal (18.5 per cent) and Italy (11.8 per cent).

Such geographical mobility results in a kind of 'psychological' distance in metropolitan life, experienced between individuals and their social and physical life. This blasé attitude is not a new phenomenon though. Georg Simmel (1903) described modern metropolitan individuals as being distinguished by an apathetic attitude which for him was a product of the 'intensification of emotional life due to the swift and uninterrupted change of outer and inner stimuli' (Simmel, 1903 [1997]:175). This creates distance, according to Simmel, as a natural or emotional reaction to the rise in the degree of 'objectification' of modern life due to the money economy. Consequently, Simmel maintained that 'we frequently do not even know by sight those who have been our neighbours for years' (Simmel, 1903 [1997]:179) as an opposing situation to what we usually encounter in non-metropolitan lifestyle (or within the southern European and Mediterranean social environment) – 'it is this reserve which in the eyes of the small-town people makes us appear to be cold and heartless' (Simmel, 1903 [1997]:179).

Secondly, Sennett referred to the marked increased standardization of the environment due to strategies that deliberately are in place to avoid the creation of a sense of belonging.

Thirdly, the increased destabilization of family life, within a wider social framework, is said to have explicitly undermined the values of loyalty and commitment at work (Sennett, 2006). In an earlier work, Sennett explored how the working experience itself underwent dramatic shifts. In *The Corrosion of Character – The Personal Consequences of Work in the New Capitalism*, Sennett (1998) made sense of generational changes in the job experiences of persons living twenty-five years apart. This work is particularly notable for embedding intergenerational accounts on work experiences within the wider socio-economic change from 'organized' to neoliberal capitalism with the increased availability of precarious jobs which leave employees with little disposable income and more prone to experience relative deprivation.

In view of this, it is no surprise that the argument that work is the route out of financial burden is highly contested by some scholars. Barbara Ehrenreich (2002) in her book *Nickel and Dimed – on (Not) Getting by in America* attacked the assumption that work is the way out of poverty. In her work she conducted covert participant observation by doing various manual jobs. She treated her working experiences in a scientific manner to test whether blue-collar work is enough to make ends meet and whether it gives you the opportunity to live above the poverty line. The assumption that low-wage jobs require an unskilled workforce was also rightfully undermined in her account. During her job experiences as a waitress, nursing assistant, maid and as a Walmart employee, she observed that all these blue-collar occupations require quick thinking, fast learning, focus and memory. Whilst harping on the lack of employment benefits in relation to health and safety, Ehrenreich (2002) aptly demonstrated that one low-wage job was insufficient to finance the minimum requirements of a person. To add up to this, the inflated housing prices make it even harder for these low earners to balance income against expenses, shaping a reality of striving hard with two and even three jobs for survival. Because of these dire conditions presented to particularly unskilled young people, Bynner and Côté (2008) stressed that 'youth have had little choice but to seek post-secondary educational credentials in the hope of gaining an advantage in access to better-paying jobs' (2008:260).

Additionally, changes in the external labour market and national systems of employment regulation resulted in greater insecurity in employments in recent years – what was referred to as the 'insecurity thesis' by Heery and Salmon (2000). This phenomenon has become ever more prominent with the advent of corporate globalization. Employees are gradually more considering themselves as insecure, partially because of the exposure of domestic markets to intense global competition. Moreover, cost reduction policies within national economies through short-term management of company assets are primarily safeguarding the financial interests of 'shareholder value'. In a globalized climate, countries are competing for the provision of good conditions to attract transnational companies (Bourdieu, 1998). Precariousness is a new mode of domination in contemporary capitalism. Building on Bourdieu's ideas, Kevin Doogan (2009), when speaking on the 'New Capitalism', has argued that the contemporary transformation of work has given rise to new employment relations, mainly characterized by a sense of precariousness and instability:

> The decline of traditional industries which offered stable and secure jobs and their replacement in a new contingent economy that offers temporary, part-time and casual work, much of which is based on flexible contracts. (Doogan, 2009:3)

The increase in involuntary job contracts, predominantly in contemporary Western societies, brought about the added risk of unemployment and reduced earnings (Heery and Salmon, 2000). On a less critical note, short-term job contracts can be considered as opportunities for different work experiences and/or offering opportunities to 'test-drive' into a particular industry and learn various skills. However, the disadvantages tend to outweigh the advantages, having youth suffering from economic and psychological effects as a result of constantly shifting jobs. It is undeniably a fact that short-term contracts create a competitive environment for individuals to compete with one another in the struggle for economic security. Most often, contract workers do not enjoy the benefit package as those occupying permanent positions. This competition, in a form of a Darwinian struggle, is fuelled by threats of restructuring and the fear of job loss.

Such trends in employment patterns were addressed in *The Disposable American* by Louis Uchitelle (2006) who noted that until the 1970s the majority of employees in America held long-term jobs. Since then, downsizing in companies resulted in a large number of persons becoming unemployed. Whereas voluntary or involuntary job changing was associated with improvement in wages in the 1960s, today changing job results in poorer working conditions and wages and increased competition.

The increase in job competition in recent years is one of the driving forces of the neoliberal system. In the name of individual sovereignty, neoliberal mechanisms built an arena where individuals compete with one another in the fight for economic security. In the face of such dilemma, young people are reaching a mutual concession and choosing courses that increase their marketability and their chances of having job stability. Young people today are negotiating their interests with the demands of the market. Competition in the job market results in individualized inclinations, having individuals work independently in their fight for job positions while in the process dissolving the sense of community. Speaking on this increased competitive nature, Beck and Beck-Gernsheim (2008[2002]:33) argued:

> Competition rests upon the interchangeability of qualifications and thereby compels people to advertise the individuality and uniqueness of their work and their own accomplishments. The growing pressure of competition leads to an individualization among equals i.e. precisely in area of interaction and conduct which are characterized by a shared background (similar education, similar experience, similar knowledge). Especially where such a shared background still exists, community is dissolved in the acid bath of competition … It causes the isolation of individuals within homogenous social groups.

The situation in the south

Out of the countries with the highest rates of youth unemployment in Europe, a number of southern European countries top the list. Notably with countries like Spain, Italy, Portugal and Greece, unemployment is a reality for almost half of the youth population. For Greece, there was no other European state in the last fifty years that has undergone such hardship due to unemployment. The economic and political crisis in Greece is said to have produced self-suffering (Tsekeris, Kaberis and Pinguli, 2015). From a macro-economic perspective, the situation of high unemployment implies low consumption and thus less revenues for public and private sectors. As a result, poverty, growing inequality and high unemployment are the everyday realities of a substantial number of young people.

In spite of efforts for EU integration and Europe's imaginative response to the new geo-political landscapes after the fall of the Berlin wall, there is still substantial north–south divide in Europe, principally in economic development. The Economic and Monetary Union (EMU) was a step forward to relegate any military conflict of the past years and aimed primarily to foster the consolidation of southern Europe's fledging democratic systems by sustaining economic growth – most significantly during the 'third wave' of democratization with Portugal, Spain and Greece joining the European Commission in the 1980s. Yet, fast-forward thirty years the situation still remains a far cry from the promised utopia (Matthijs, 2014).

After civil wars, there were still dictatorships and colonialism in southern Europe until the mid-1970s. During the industrialization processes of most southern European countries, attention was placed on high protective employment regimes including the stringent employment protection legislation as a legacy of the authoritarian/corporatist ideologies influencing policymakers. In countries like Portugal, Greece and Spain, democratic governments that took power during the 1970s and 1980s abstained from dismantling the labour legislation of previous authoritarian past due to fears of social unrest (Karamessini, 2008). Highly protective employment legislations, especially against the dismissal of workers from core sectors of the economy, guaranteed a family wage and high job stability to the typically male workforce.

With the rise in unemployment in the late 1970s and early 1980s, southern European countries launched labour deregulation reforms. For Portuguese and Spanish governments measures were in place to facilitate the unrestricted use of fixed-term contracts. As a result, there was an increase in temporary employment and the reinforcement of labour market segmentation (Marí-Klose and Moreno-Fuentes, 2013).

As for the Greek and Italian governments, reforms implemented for fixed-term contracts were more limited and their implications less severe. During times of economic slowdown, temporary workers were forced to shoulder labour readjustment measures. In Spain, the economic crisis in the beginning of the 1990s increased youth unemployment rates.

Southern European countries experienced high levels of unemployment particularly during the Great Recession in the late 2000s. In Greece, Spain, Portugal and Italy, 6 million paid jobs were lost between 2007 and 2013, with Greece and Spain which experienced the loss of one job out of every five (Gutiérrez, 2014). Such changes brought with them a sudden increase in income inequality and an upsurge rate of poverty.

In the last decade, various southern European countries experienced further financial hardship and direct financial assistance by the European Union. The so-called 'troika' was a widely used term to refer to financial measures by, International Monetary Fund (IMF) and the European Commission and their presence to respond to sovereign-debt crisis in countries like Greece, Cyprus, Ireland Portugal and Spain. Various changes in the 'Mediterranean variant' of welfare capitalism in the last two decades had noteworthy effects on employment opportunities (Ferrera, 1996, 2005, Petmesidou and Papatheodorou, 2006). Despite the strong recovery after the global financial crisis in 2008 and the world recession in 2009, most southern European countries showed signs of recovery; yet, one of the lasting economic damage was still the relatively high rate of unemployment.

There is a clear correlation between the level of young people with lowest level of qualifications and their chances of unemployment in places like Greece, Spain, Italy and Portugal (Gutiérrez, 2014). Rodolfo Gutiérrez examined three groups of young people, one from each educational level and in an appropriate age group to allow adequate labour integration time since leaving the education system. These included the 20–24-year-old cohort who finished compulsory education, the 25–29-year-old cohort who completed the post-compulsory level and the 30–35-year-old cohort who experienced tertiary education.

Irrespective of this correlation, the employment rate of recent graduates by educational attainment in most southern European countries remains below the EU average of (80.2 per cent) – Greece (52 per cent), Italy (55.2 per cent), Spain (71.9 per cent). Portugal is just above the average at 80.7 per cent and Malta is an exception to the rule, with an employment rate of recent graduates at 94.5 per cent (European Commission, 2018).

Because of such low job prospects for graduates, there is a growing inclination for migration flows amongst highly qualified youth in countries with high unemployment and austerity measures. For instance, in Greece and Italy, highly qualified youth feel deprived of opportunities at their respective home countries and are prone to explore new professional opportunities abroad (Triandafyllidou and Gropas, 2007).

Another vital factor in the labour market in southern European countries is the low rate of female paid employment, with most countries having the lowest rates within the EU, with the exception of Portugal. Compared to men, women's rate of unemployment in the Greece, Italy, Portugal and Spain remains higher. There is also a substantial gender pay gaps compared to other EU states. These work practices in the South are influenced not only by economic processes but also by cultural conditions, including the persistence of family farming, family businesses, self-employment and the industrial restricting processes resulting in high levels of informal work, which often remain invisible in official statistics (Cousins, 2000). This is discussed thoroughly in Chapter 5.

Conclusion

With shifts in the labour market, especially in the last few decades, young people are increasingly facing a rather juddering ride in their transition from school to work. This chapter explored changes in the labour market and their direct implications on life-course transitions towards adulthood, often measured in terms of the school-to-work transition. Such changes at work, from the promise of a 'job for life' to more flexible work conditions, were addressed in line with the macro-socio-economic changes since the late 1950s – from the so-called 'organized capitalism' to a neoliberal form. Following this analysis, it is worth exploring a micro-overview on the implications of this shift in the everyday lives of youth with tertiary education.

4
Neoliberal intersubjectivity: A way of doing things

Some of the distinctive characteristics of how young people are leading an individualized lifestyle include the way they are operating autonomously as entrepreneurial selves and how they have embodied a kind of neoliberal application to their self. 'Neoliberalism has pervasive effects on ways of thought' claimed David Harvey (2005:3) predominantly in an age when neoliberalism became a 'scientific description of reality' (Bourdieu, 1998:94). It is considered as a 'doxa', an objective truth across the social space, wisely crafted as the inevitable truth of the social world. Because of the fact that millennials were trained under neoliberal conditions, they are often casual and phlegmatic about it and treat it as a 'natural' mode of life. The neoliberal self is made flexible in terms of working conditions and adapts easily to changes to meet market demands (du Gay, 1996, Boltanski and Chiapello, 2006, Sennett, 1998, 2006).

Discourses on self-development and self-fashioning entrepreneurship are proof of the workings of neoliberalism on the individual. The intensification of neoliberalism in everyday life, or what is known as the neoliberal subjectivity, is well documented (Rose, 1999, Walkerdine, 2003, Türken et al., 2016), especially in the way it is now ubiquitously influencing all spheres of life through a form of branding of the self (O'Flynn and Petersen, 2007, Gill, 2008, Hochschild and Garrett, 2011).

This chapter builds an understanding of how the neoliberal ideology works on subjectivity and in the way this mind frame is often considered as hardly ever contested and taken as an inevitable part of living today. The grounds for consent is based on the process of cultural socialization that generates the feeling that it is the only common sense choice – a reality that 'gives the dominant discourse its strength' (Bourdieu, 1998:30). By using the media effectively and seeking the approval of intellectuals, neoliberal thinkers propagated this myth making it conventional wisdom that 'there is no alternative' to this economic philosophy.

This chapter focuses on the promotion of individual initiative and how it runs parallel to the increased weight put on self-reliance and neoliberal governmentality. In tandem with the shifts from state responsibility onto the individual and the dismantling of the welfare state, individuals are more than ever responsible for their own success due to 'a programme of methodical destruction of collectives' (Bourdieu, 1998:95–96). Thus, this chapter explores the process to how the self is more than ever interpreted in terms of one's 'reflexive biography' instead of a socially produced entity.

Additionally, this chapter builds on what Jim McGuigan (2010) has said on the kind of subjectivity in neoliberal globalization, by referring to a type of individual that is very much attuned to living in such economic conditions today:

> The popular appeal of neoliberalism.. is similarly [to individualisation] experienced as liberating, albeit that this is somewhat illusory; for everyone, freedom of choice and opportunity to make it on your own. (McGuigan, 2010:110–111)

To explore this kind of embodiment of neoliberalism on the self for millennials, it is useful to first examine the structure of feeling of this generation as the culture of a period shaping subjectivities and lived experiences.

The structure of feeling of millennials

To make sense of the subjective neoliberal self of millennials, I'm borrowing Raymond Williams's remarkable decription on the 'structure of feeling' produced by a generation (Williams, 1961[1965]). It is about an understanding of any social formation through examining social practices and taken-for-granted behaviour and beliefs of a generation.

In *The Long Revolution* Williams described this by saying:

It is as firm and definite as "structure" suggests, yet it operates in the most delicate and least tangible parts of our activity. In one sense, this structure of feeling is the culture of a period: it is the particular living result of all the elements in the general organisation. And it is in this respect that the arts of a period, taking these to include characteristics approaches and tones in argument, are of major importance. For here, if anywhere, this characteristic is likely to be expressed; often not consciously, but by the fact that here in the only examples we have of recorded communication that outlives its bearers, the actual living sense, the deep community that makes the communication possible, is naturally drawn upon. (Williams, 1961[1965]:64–65)

In his later work *Marxism and Literature*, Williams (1977) maintained that one should understand culture in terms of past and future aspirations as well as the present lived experiences of a generation.

A casual observation on our everyday experiences tells us how we are saturated with emotions that are structured in relation to the particular period. Albeit the generic affirmative feelings of excitement, free spirit and anticipation associated with youth as a life course, the application of this 'structure of feeling' for millennials is studied here by referring to three shared adverse feelings of this generation: the feeling of anxiety, the feeling of resentment and the feeling of pessimism.

First, feelings of anxiety, due to increased uncertainties, are attenuated in the 'fluid' living conditions within the so-called liquid modernity. Zygmunt Bauman (2000, 2007, 2011), in his series of books, has compellingly argued on the restless 'liquid' lifestyle in late capitalism with increased flexible and self-fashioning 'entrepreneurial subjects' (du Gay, 1996). For Bauman people are nomads, flowing through changing situations and identities, and facing uncertainties and growing anxieties in 'fluid' situations. However, it warrants to mention that the feeling of anxiety is far from a new condition experienced only by the millennial generation – it is an intrinsic part of youth as a life course in transition. More than a century ago, Stanley Hall (1904) considered youth as a period of 'storm and stress' not only because individuals experience biological developments during puberty but also due to socially constructed developments that typify this stage. To some degree, the risk behaviour is associated with identity exploration and the desire for new intense experiences in sensation seeking. Youth is a stage prevalent of depressed moods rooted in friendships and intimate relationships. Hall (1904) explained this in terms of the transitory phase of adolescence as causing 'suspicion of being disliked by friends, of having faults of person or character that cannot be overcome, the fancy of ... hopeless love' (1904:78).

Sixty years later, Ferdynand Zweig (1963) in *The Student in the Age of Anxiety* highlighted some of the apprehensions experienced by university students at that time. He referred to the stress of university life and the anxiety of youth in relation to work prospects and personal relations. The political atmosphere during this time was also causing trepidation, having Russia threatening American society with a nuclear attack. During the cold war in the 1960s, the possibility of a nuclear war became more real for apprehensive youth. During times when superpowers in the East and West were testing powerful new weapon, young people in the 1960s lived through constant fear of total human annihilation. They witnessed the rise of the Iron Curtain which intensified threats of mass destruction. The possibility of nuclear destruction haunted their dreams.

In more recent years, anxiety is believed to have heightened by increased risk in society – 'apprehension is created in a climate emphasizing constant risk, and apprehension increases when past experience seems no guide to the present' (Sennett, 1998:97). To some degree, risk behaviour is associated with identity exploration in youth and the desire for new intense experiences in sensation seeking. The increased reflexivity in personal identity allowing choice in late modernity is considered as one of the main causes for anxiety: 'Identity is increasingly a matter of choice and a reflexively organised endeavour' (Giddens, 1991:5).

In *Risk Society*, Ulrich Beck (1992) sustained that by the end of the twentieth century, we have witnessed a historical transformation. The predictabilities and certainties of the industrial era were now threatened and the Western world is constantly confronted with risk. With the freedom from traditional constraints and social networks, as well as the demise of some of the agents of security, risk is now negotiated in our everyday lives, in a world that is gradually perceived as a dangerous place. Risk is also unequally distributed in society and follows the inequalities of a class society:

> Like wealth, risk adhere to the class pattern, only inversely: wealth accumulates at the top, risks at the bottom. To that extent, risks seem to *strengthen*, not abolish, the class society. Poverty attracts an unfortunate abundance of risks. By contrast, the wealthy (in income, power or education) can *purchase* safety and freedom from risk. (Beck, 1992:35)

Various social theorists built on Beck's study to understand how risk is constructed, avoided and measured. Deborah Lupton (1999), for instance, traced how risk has become prominent in late modernity by looking at how it was constructed over time. She addressed three epistemological positions on risk – a realist position where risk is objective and measurable, the weak constructionist position in which risk is objective but mediated through social and cultural processes, and the strong constructionist position where nothing is risky but a product of history and social political forces. Risk is also considered as part of a progressive process for enterprise and for the creation of wealth. Despite that risk is linked to a feeling of uneasiness, it is also seen as an invaluable part for development, a source or condition of opportunity for progress (O'Malley, 1996).

The feeling of apprehension associated with risk is accentuated by the shift from state to personal responsibility, specifically when the individual is blamed for personal failure like unemployment (Beck, 1992). With 'precarious freedoms', young people are expected to fashion their own futures through their decisions as neoliberal agents regardless of the unequal playing field and shoulder responsibility for their own failures. In this regard, increased choice and freedom in the ability to act on one's own calculations yet as a consequence increased risk and uncertainties.

As we are bound to experience increased risk in late modernity, all certainties of transcendence, including in love, are arguably lost. In the *Normal Chaos of Love*, Ulrich Beck and Elisabeth Beck-Gernsheim (1995[1990]) move beyond the accusation of personal failure when speaking about fractured love relationships and embed the complications in close relationships in the transformation of family life. Marital relations are said to have acquired new meaning in the individualized society. One reason Beck and Beck-Gernsheim (2008 [2002]) gave for this shift in the attitudes towards marriage is the rise in complexities and biological uncertainties in youth. The increased choices and alternatives on how to devise one's own life, and with whom to share it with, brought forward a feeling of uncertainty and the normalization of moving out of a non-functional relationship. This contrasts with the meanings and feelings associated to the institution of marriage for baby boomers. Marriage was practically a 'natural' rite of passage into adulthood and habitually it was hardly regarded as a real option. Marriage was not so much based on self-discovery but it was anchored in religious obligation, in serving God and the community (Visanich, 2012).

Furthermore, the added stress put on self-discovery and a more secularized orientation to life shifted the meaning of life and death; death is more than ever interpreted as an end, an absolute and irrevocable end. Dying is a threat to one's own life and thus this produces anxiety for those alive to have full control of how to live their life, with persistent pressures to 'live life to the full' as a constant struggle against time. In *Time Bind*, Arlie Russell Hochschild (1997) referred to this notion of time when saying how today individuals

> speak of time as if it was a threatened form of personal capital they have no choice but to manage and invest, capital whose value seems to rise and fall according to forces beyond their control. (1997:51)

Second, the feeling of resentment is another shared feeling by millennials in their relationship with older generations. This 'structure of feeling' is best understood when examining the implicit social contract between generations, in this case between the baby boomers versus the millennials. Because of demographic changes, with an increase in life span and lower birth rates, there has been a substantial impact on intergenerational relationships. Older people are extending their working years and thus the replenishment of the workforce by the younger generation has stalled (Bynner and Côté, 2008). What's more, the tug of war for the allocation of resources is continuously building up tension amongst the working population and the baby boomers as they enter retirement and become part of the welfare-dependent population. This is one causal factor for fuelling tension between generations: While the baby boomers are guaranteed state pensions, it is less likely that millennials will be state supported during their third age.

This presumed generational conflict was aptly explored by Anya Kamenetz (2007) when dubbing the 'young' elderly as the 'greediest generation' who are receiving their pensions, paid by the present working generation, whereas the latter cannot secure themselves a career. In a recent newspaper article *'Millennials Are Struggling. Is It the Fault of Babyboomers?'* Yvonne Roberts (2018) interrogated these generational inequalities in view of the great mismatch of life chances of the baby boomers compared to the millennials. She dubs the generation of the baby boomers as 'toxic', because of the greed and selfishness in denying the younger generation the same benefits they enjoyed, including affordable housing and a pension.

The implications of this are serious to a point that it required setting up a commission to investigate in-depth the situation and come up with measures to counteract generational inequalities. The 'Intergenerational Commission for Resolution Foundation' (2019) in Britain published a report on these intergenerational disparities by investigating the lived experiences of both generations. The commission addressed the inequity in resources available for the two generations; yet, it also acknowledged the betterment in the standards of living of young people today compared to their older counterparts.

Third, according to recent surveys, the feeling of pessimism about the future is noticeably growing amongst youth. Britain, just like Greece, is considered the most pessimistic country amongst the advanced economic countries, with a shared mood that has significant implications on the well-being of individuals (Weale, 2018). Specifically, young persons aged between eighteen and twenty-four happen to be the most pessimistic age cohort in the UK, with only one in seven thinking that their age group will have opportunities for social mobility. Just 13 per cent of this age cohort believe that they will enjoy better standards of living and live financially better off than older generations (Social Mobility Commission, 2018).

This pessimism is equally experienced by millennials with tertiary education in Greece. This is partly the result of Greece's current toughest job market in the developed world, with youth unemployment as high as 40 per cent within a decade-long financial crisis. As part of the 'BBC Generation Project', journalist Jessica Bateman (2018) documents the lives of graduates in Greece and their experiences of being redundant and working a series of short-term, low-skilled jobs after graduation. A 28-year-old graduate in Political Sciences interviewed participant has said:

> My friends and I were all very anxious about finding a job related to our studies, and whether this job would even be permanent. I was lucky because I could live with my parents, but for those who had to live alone it was extremely hard. (Bateman, 2018, BBC Generation Project online)

This economic hardship is one of the reasons why around 250,000 graduates have left Greece to look for employment in other countries over the past eight years (Bateman, 2018). Greece in recent history experienced strikes and protests that brought the country to a standstill particularly in 2011, when a 109-billion euro bailout was agreed. Officially Greece exited this bailout programme in August 2018 with hopes of GDP growth by 2.32 per cent in 2019 (Bateman, 2018).

Unstable economic conditions do not only generate pessimism but also have a psychological toll, especially on young people who want to enter the job market. Economic changes and shifts in welfare policies, in the last sixty years, had significant implications on the structuring of feelings of youth and how these are played out in their everyday lives. Such feelings for millennials are increasingly pooled through policy systems that encourage individual rather than state responsibility. The heavy restructuring of the welfare state, especially in pensions, is one of the multi-causalities for cross-generational pessimism and apprehension about future prospects for young adults.

Changes from collective to individual: From welfare ideology to neoliberal subjectivity

'There is no such thing as society', proclaimed Margaret Thatcher in 1987 to sustain her argument on the growing emphasis on self-interested individuals rather than groups. Millennials are the first generation of youth who grew up in a market-based society grounded in the principles of self-interest and competition as opposed to communal interest and civic responsibility. The neoliberal ideology had worked to fray collective bonds and welfare programmes in its promotion of self-reliance instead of interdependent citizens. These conditions contrast heavily the state intervention measures and the increase in the social wage during organized capitalism in the post-Second World War, as explained in the previous chapter on the provision of full employment. However, the expansion in state welfare was addressed not only in education and employment policies but also in other measures to combat poverty. The two British White Papers, the 'Family Allowance Act' and the 'National Insurance Act', in 1944 were a step forward to guarantee social inclusion and combat poverty. An allowance for every child and benefits for those unemployed, sick or widowed safeguarded citizens from the risk of poverty (Jones, 2005[2000]). At the same time, a commitment to offer comprehensive health services was protected via a National Health Service Act in Britain. Services free of charge were intended to overcome diseases through the prevention, diagnosis and treatment of illness.

It was a popular belief that the government intervened by measures aimed at redistribution of resources and focused on delivering economic growth and employment. In one of the most prominent books on post-war British Labour Party thinking *The Future of Socialism*, Anthony Crosland (1956) maintained that there was no need to nationalize the private sector if appropriate interventions were implemented along the Keynesian practice. He regarded nationalization as one possible 'means' to an 'end' for improving society (Crosland, 1956). He asserted that equality of opportunity needed to be balanced by increasing social welfare and equality in the distribution of rewards and privileges in an attempt to diminish class distinctions. This was central to his argument on the continuation of improvement of the welfare services for the provision of egalitarian reforms in the education system and the distribution of property.

As opposed to Keynes's state interventionist theories, contemporary economic practices in Western societies are more commonly touted as tearing social relations. Emphasis is laid on individual freedom and free market as a prerequisite for a liberal society. Framed within this ideology, neoliberal policies dismantled state interventions such as public services and the breaking of unions whilst placing the burden on personal responsibilities. Reform of the welfare state included policies for 'replacing social welfare systems by private insurance schemes and private pension funds' (Gorz, 1999:20). The neoliberal ideology challenged the view that the state should provide for one's welfare including in old age. Policymakers are particularly questioning the cost of having an ageing population. It is becoming conventional wisdom in the West that the state should not provide pensions above a minimum rate due to its unsustainability but instead promote individual responsibility and put pressure on young generations to invest in private pension provisions – thus disseminating the individualist belief that you have to take care for yourself and plan your future wisely. This kind of individual orientation is also manifested in the way young people are more than ever prone to embody a kind of neoliberal entrepreneurial self through personal branding.

Personal branding and the culture of perfectionism

> Personal branding advocates consistently stress a positive outlook consistent with both the portrayal of economic turmoil as inevitable and the call to American-style self-reliance: To give in to the turbulence is to accept defeat; to lose faith in one's ability to succeed is to give up on the American dream. Cynicism, then, is not an option; it can only prevent one from succeeding.
> (Lair, Sullivan and Cheney, 2005:324)

A simple keyword search for the term 'personal branding' results in a myriad of choices in books, magazines, training courses and personal coaching to teach oneself into building a personal brand, designed and packaged for a successful career. Personal branding is about a set of semiotics techniques to promote hyper-individuality, especially within the employment market. It is a way of an ongoing process of establishing an impression of oneself, in a kind of self-commodification exchange within a neoliberal market. It validates how neoliberalism is related to subjectivity in the way neoliberal measures take on culture and identity. In many forms, the personal branding as a concept shares affinities with the self-couching movement as it offers a tool-kit through practices and strategies on how individuals can improve themselves within the competitive job market. However, personal branding deals also with self-packaging – a brand which gives an individual a competitive edge and a proactive response to a target audience over others.

Personal branding emerged as a movement in consonant with the intensification of globalization explicitly within the arenas of competition, at a time when increased emphasis is placed on the individual to compete in the corporate world. Despite increased globalization, equally important phenomena are the increased localization and community-oriented variances, and personalization. The intersections of these are treated as having a central position in the branding of the self and a business. In view of this, it is notable to address discourse on globalization and glocalization in the understanding of the self and how it is presented in everyday life.

It is conventional wisdom that Western globalization created a global culture of sameness and uniformity as well as coherence, reliability and certainty, whilst dissolving in the process the diversity of authentic cultures. This viewpoint, mostly emphasizing the pervasiveness of Western culture (Lieber and Weisberg, 2002), suggests the loss of cultural diversity, in which the local and authentic disappears in the ambush of cultural homogenization processes (Schirato and Webb, 2003). This is mostly exemplified in the argument on the core/periphery relations whereby the core centre allegedly dominates the periphery (Featherstone, 1995).

Such a supposition perceives local communities as being powerless or insignificant. This viewpoint is strongly opposed due to the intersection of cultural influences from dominant political powers and local cultures. Global cultural influences are regarded as becoming indigenized within local communities (Appadurai, 1990). It is indeed an assumption, or as described by Marjorie Ferguson (1992) in her academic paper title 'the Mythology about Globalisation', to regard such process as a large-scale cultural homogenizing force, overriding the local. The meaning, evidence and evaluation of globalization are challenged critically by Ferguson (1992) as she explored seven myths about this notion – the myth that 'Big is Better', 'More is Better', 'Time and Space Have Disappeared', 'Global Cultural Homogeneity', 'Saving Planet Earth', 'Democracy for Export via American TV' and 'The New World Order'. In line with this Roland Robertson (1990) argued that

> the distinction between the global and the local is becoming very complex and problematic – to such an extent that we should now speak in such terms as the global institutionalization of the life-world and the localization of globality. (1990:17)

Having its roots in Japan, the concept of glocalization is closely related to micro-marketing within the business marketing sphere. It is defined as having its scope based on 'the tailoring and advertising of goods and services on a global or near-global basis to increasingly differentiated local and particular markets' (Robertson, 1995:28). He extended the use of this concept to refer and highlight the importance of local cultural identities when conceptualizing the global. The global is not seen here in opposition of the local; instead, the local is an aspect of the global. The localization of the global, therefore, refers to the interrelationships and complementarities of the global with the local – a notion which parallels Appardurai's (1990) concept of hybridity.

Despite the glocal characteristics of the neoliberal self, there are certain common transversal features which cannot be ignored. These include individual efficacy, identity and control. It is a form of consolidation between the marketing culture with the initially American individual dream of success through mastering one's own destiny (Lair, Sullivan and Cheney, 2005). Without a doubt, personal branding works hand-in-hand with the production of a 'perfect' self and the prospect of 'stardom' which can reach its full potential by unlocking inner fortes in a culture where 'the sky is the limit'. This kind of 'celebrity democracy', as Jim McGuigan (2009) calls it, deals with the presumed attainable role of celebrity or pseudo-aristocracy culture pioneered by the Hollywood star system. It perpetuates the myth that everyone can achieve stardom and its desired fame and fortune, with their own hard work and effort. Richard Dyer (1977) looked into the dynamics of celebrity in his book *Stars*, by referring to how 'stars ... are the direct or indirect reflection of the needs, drives and dreams of American society' (Dyer, 1977:6). Related to stardom is the false assumption of democratization of fame and fortune through perfectionism by means of hard work.

Perfectionism is fittingly defined as 'the tyranny of the should' (Horney, 1950:64). Living in a market-based society, young people have growing demands for excellence on how to perform in their everyday life and they also demand more from others (Curran and Hill, 2019). They are more than ever being sifted, sorted and ranked by the educational system, their employers and their peers. Digital mobile devices and the use of social media like Instagram, Facebook and Snapchat are continuously used as forms of connectivity to peers. Yet, they also act as platforms for exchange curations for self-perfection with the affirmation for likes. This is all within a context where it is hard to come across a photo which hasn't been filtered and photoshopped into a simulacra of flawlessness. Such conditions feed insecurities particularly amongst young people and shape how they should behave, look and what they should own to attain a desired self in terms of what is considered hip. Young people are more or less circumspect in their presentation of a 'distinctive' self and their association with their peers.

> Millennials are interacting all day but almost entirely through a screen. You've seen them at bars, sitting next to one another and texting. They might look calm, but they're deeply anxious about missing out on something better. Seventy per cent of them check their phones every hour, and many experience phantom pocket-vibration syndrome. "They're doing a behaviour to reduce their anxiety," says Larry Rosen, a psychology professor. (Stein, 2013, *Time* magazine online)

The culture of perfectionism requires daunting incessant entrepreneurial self-work. Perfectionism for psychologists is a multidimensional concept. The various self-development and life coaching sessions popularized today to stimulate conscious, rational subjects shed light on the importance given to attain one's full potential in contemporary society. Gaining reflexivity, self-awareness and being in touch with one self are considered as drivers towards achieving a state of perfectionism.

For Thomas Curran and Andrew Hill (2019), there are three types of perfectionism: the self-oriented, the other-oriented and the socially prescribed. Whereas the self-oriented perfectionism puts oneself to an unrealistically high standard, the other-oriented have unrealistic expectations of others. However, the socially prescribed one is about a feeling of anxiety of not being good enough; yet, one persists to the others' impossible expectations at the expense of overwhelming anxiety and paranoia. Curran and Hall (2019) examined the direct relationship between cultural change after the 1980s, with emphasis on competitive individualism, the increased levels of perfectionism and its association with serious mental illness. It is quite telling that young people today are suffering more from depression, anxiety and eating disorders compared to their predecessors.

This is one of the implications of living in a neoliberal society, what Curran and Hall (2019) refer to as 'neoliberal meritocracy' – a situation that created a cutthroat environment in which every person becomes commodified as their own brand ambassador in a highly competitive environment.

This personal neoliberal mode of life promotes ambition and tethers personal worth to professional achievement. It is a mode of life constantly in search for meticulousness on a fast-moving treadmill. Consequentially, it is changing fundamentally the way millennials view themselves and others. Psychologists Paul Hewitt, Gordon Flett and Samuel Mikail (2017) delve into the development of perfectionism and its underlying mechanisms in the changing self-perception and often harsh self-criticism of unworthiness. The drivers to attain perfection are the irrational desires to be flawless especially in a climate where performance, status and your presentation of the self define your usefulness.

Conclusion

The 'structure of feeling' is not only constructed in terms of the specific cultural milieu of a generation but also framed within wider social structures including economic conditions. This chapter explored these feelings and how they are shaping the ideology of a neoliberal application on the self as self-fashioning entrepreneurs. It is of particular interest in this book to explore how this way of thinking and presentation of the self is adopted in southern European locations. The next chapter builds on this by taking into consideration the cultural particularities in southern European countries which cushion some of youths' challenges experienced in everyday life that were mentioned in previous chapters.

5

Shock-Absorbers for youth in the South

Ulrich Beck (1992) was not completely right when he said that processes of reflexive modernization 'tend to dissolve' the traditional conditions of industrial society. Essentially, this is not really the case in southern Europe. It bears much truth to say that youth in southern countries are not completely released from such conditions including those related to class, gender and familialism – referring to the family taking on the responsibility and welfare of its members.

In recent years, comparative research on social policy in the southern region provided a model on the prominent role of traditional structures including the strong and resilient family, as an inevitable form of social insurance safeguarding against poverty and social exclusion. Socio-political and economic comparisons are useful in the South but insufficient to grasp thoroughly the specificities of this region. It is well documented that there are other characteristics of southern countries which distinguish them, including their historical and cultural commonalities (Gal, 2010), the influence of religion (in particular Catholicism) in all aspects of social life as well as the central role of the family and the presence of 'familism' (family solidarity and dependency). Nonetheless, it is not the scope here to treat the South as homogenous but rather to highlight certain common characteristics and their impact on the life experiences of young adults.

This chapter unpacks the cultural cushioning system in southern Europe and explores how this eases the transition from youth into adulthood. It is not only the rather decommodified welfare model that is cushioning citizens but also family kinship ties. Explicitly, this chapter looks at the familialism, kinship patterns and cultural conditions in traditional families in southern European countries like Italy, Spain, Portugal and Malta and makes sense of how these function as 'shock-absorbers', as considered by Maurizio Ferrera (2010), cushioning members from short-term deprivations like unemployment and family breakdown.

> The family has historically been the cornerstone of South European societies, functioning as an effective 'social shock absorber' and welfare broker for its members and responding to a wide range of risks and needs, from childcare to unemployment, from care for the elderly to disabled and housing. (Ferrera, 2010:622)

The 'family question' is central in this regard in the understanding of the allocation of family responsibilities as the main feature of welfare state models. The tendency for resource pooling and intergenerational financial and emotional support, especially taking prime responsibility in times of sickness and dependency, is backed by the social doctrine of the Catholic Church (and the Greek Orthodox Church which plays a functionally equivalent role) as a central cultural influencer in the lives of members of society. In effect, the South tells us a lot about the complex relationship between the state, the market and the role of the family – all as the three main cornerstones of the welfare model.

This chapter also examines general tendencies in the lived experiences of youth in the South including the extension in the period of economic dependence on their parents, at times perceived as rooted in an over-nurturing mentality. The longevity in years spent in education and training, partly due to high unemployment, as well as the increase in short-term contract jobs have had considerable impact on the transition of young people into independent living. Prolonging of partial dependence of youth is also the consequence of the increase in house prices over recent decades. The ability to have an independent lifestyle at a young age in a separate dwelling became harder to access particularly in the last two decades.

This chapter also looks at the personal agency of female millennials in southern Europe who are said to be more autonomous than previous generations of women. Individualized young women are increasingly choosing how to devise their own life projects and work out their ideas about the future. Yet still, cultural conditions in the South continuously play an important role in the life prospects of women. Living within a culture of persistent gender inequality, a visible glass ceiling and substantial gender pay gap, there is still a considerable disproportion in employment and opportunities patterns for men and women in this region.

Welfare provisions in the South

Despite differences in timing, welfare provisions in Mediterranean countries share some commonalities based on their similar cultural heritage. These include resemblances in the labour market, its predominance of the male breadwinner as well as the strong reliance on the family for the provision of basic economic security and care for members (Gutiérrez, 2014). Unlike in other Western countries the shifts from welfare state support to a more privatized neoliberal market-oriented welfare model were less straightforward in southern European countries. A decommodified system of National Health Service is common in these countries (Saraceno, 1994). Therefore, it is right to say that social welfare provisions in the South are not completely an endangered concept.

Herein by welfare model, I am referring to an explanatory rather than descriptive definition by taking account of similarities and differences amongst countries as evidence of contrasting clusters which are based on various criteria. These include issues on political economy, decommodification and social stratification. In view of this, it is useful to draw from Gøsta Esping-Andersen's notion of welfare state regimes which rests on the postulation that 'in the relation between state and economy a complex of legal and organisational features is systematically interwoven' (Esping-Andersen, 1990:2). Esping-Andersen (1990) was one of the first scholars to speak about the particularities of countries like Spain, Italy and Greece in terms of a conservative welfare regime, as opposed to countries like Germany, Austria and the Netherlands. His view of the decommodification model is based on state social welfare provisions. Yet Esping-Andersen's decommodification welfare model leaves out important factors worth considering (Pereirinha, 1997). Primarily, such model excludes the informal labour market which has a substantial presence in the South. This model also ignores mechanisms of social solidarity and informal institutions, such as the Catholic Church with its various organizations that work to combat poverty and social exclusion in society. It is equally important to say that most welfare models in the South are truly a hybrid of models which do not fit neatly in one particular model of welfare as outlined by Esping-Andersen (1990).

All southern European countries are said to have a mix of universalist healthcare systems with the provision of state pension schemes (Guillén, 1996). For Maurizio Ferrera (2000) the southern model is a mix of 'occupationalism' (maintenance system) and 'universalism' (health service) that is atypical in other parts in Europe.

> While displaying high institutional fragmentation along occupational lines in their income maintenance systems, the Southern European welfare states are characterised by a universalistic approach in their health care systems .... The mix between income maintenance occupationalism and health care universalism is a quite peculiar trait of the welfare state of this area of Europe. (Ferrera, 2000:169)

Thus, with respect to other systems of social protection, southern welfare states are considered to be a *via media* because they encompass both elements of Bismarckian and Beveridgian traditions (Moreno, 1997). It is an attention-grabbing fact that all southern European countries are just below the European Union (EU) average when it comes to social protection expenditure; compared to the EU28 average (2017) of 18.8 per cent, Spain (16.6 per cent), Portugal (17.4 per cent) and Malta (11.3 per cent) have a below-average rate, with Italy (20.9 per cent) being the exception (Eurostat, 2019e). In view of the relatively paucity of Social Protection expenditure predominantly in some areas such as housing, it is inevitable to address the role of the civil society, families and the voluntary sector, by stressing both material and non-material intra-familial transfers, for the provision of social protection. Cultural conditions, including the vital role of the family, as a source for solidarity and dependency, and the influence of religion (in particular Catholicism) in all aspects of social life, are central for welfare provisions to citizens. Accordingly, the role of the informal support family network changes substantially the understanding of the functioning of the welfare state.

Catholic-oriented values are given a central position in the southern European family (Guerrero and Naldini, 1997). Religious institutions, acting as socialization agents, play a relatively crucial role in shaping young people's experiences and dispositions. Church intellectuals work as educators primarily by rooting the ideology of the Roman Catholic Church at a very early age. As a consequence, this relatively shapes the dispositions as well as the life expectations and trajectories of members in southern European societies. Evidence of this is the importance given to the voluntary sector in southern European countries, in particular in voluntary religious groups as one of the Catholic ethics of community orientation as opposed to the more individualist Protestant ethics.

There is a sharp difference in western and southern youth in their affiliation to an organized religion. For instance, Bynner and Côté (2008) referred to Canadian statistics that reported that youth are less affiliated to an organized religion (40 per cent of twenty-four years or younger were not affiliated to a religion). With these outcomes, they maintained that organized religion is continuing to decline in its normative influence in the transition to adulthood, and therefore it is becoming less of an important source for adult identity. In contrast, in more traditional religious backgrounds like in southern European countries, religious training is still a significant part of the socialization process. This effects various dispositions in one's life. An example of this is in the strong sense of obligation that family members have for each other which is somewhat rooted in the Catholic doctrine.

While doing extensive anthropological studies in Malta, the Dutch anthropologist Jeremy Boissevain (2006) outlined the interplay between the family and the Roman Catholic religion in Malta. Whilst examining Maltese society in the 1960s, Boissevain gave a vivid description of the family at that time. Marriage was (and still is in a way) not only considered as a 'natural' process but as a rite of passage to a distinctive patriarchal division of roles for males and females. It is conventional wisdom that the husband/father is the breadwinner, with the responsibility to provide food and shelter whilst the wife/mother is to produce children and 'train [them] for the service of Christ' (Boissevain, 2006:17).

Family formation and kinship ties

With recent changes in the family form and function in the Anglo-American context, it is quite challenging today to find a universally agreed definition of what constitutes the family. As explained in previous chapters, traditional life-course transitions to adulthood are said to have become increasingly broken down into interconnected events, with no specific chronological order. The lengthening years in education coupled with the increased demand for short-term contract jobs led to a more fragmented life-course transitions (Lasch, 1991, Sennett, 1998, Beck and Beck-Gernsheim, 2008[2002], Ehrenreich, 2002, Kamenetz, 2007).

The event of household formation, for example, has become separate from family formation. Principally, marriage and living arrangements also underwent dramatic changes. Legal alternative to marriage, such as un/registered partnership, has become widespread and young people are more free to choose the type of partnership that fits them best. In effect, the predominance of the lack of normative organizational stages in human lives is mostly evident with the de-institutionalization of marriage in the twentieth-first century. With the increased rate of cohabitation and reconstituted arrangements, joint households are no longer only tied by marital relationships. Moreover, the increased rates of divorce are shifting life courses, because in some cases divorcees are returning back to their parental home.

Marital relations have acquired new meanings in the individualized society. The reorganization of work is fostering the need for a sense of belonging for individuals – a need that was previously provided by the family. In her study, Arlie Hochschild (1997) referred to a new model of family and work life that is making individuals feel 'at home' when they are at work while making them estranged to their family life. She addressed this predominant 'reversal' pattern that is shaping the way individuals look at work and family life. Family life is becoming less satisfying for individuals, and rather than seen in terms of obligation it is considered as an option that they can break free from at work.

For those who are choosing to get married, there is a tendency for delaying this rite of passage to late twenties and early thirties. The average marriage age for men in countries of the EU stands at 29.8, whereas for women it is 27.4 years. Likewise, the age at which women give birth to her first child has also been delayed – now reaching an average age of 29.1 years of women in the EU in 2017, ranging from 26.1 in Bulgaria to 31.1 in Italy (Eurostat, 2019c). There are noteworthy differences in fertility rates in different countries in Europe.

Families in northern Europe (Sweden, Denmark and Norway) tend to have relatively high fertility rates and divorce incidences as well as higher levels of cohabitation and births outside wedlock. This contrasts trends in families in the South (Portugal, Spain, Italy and Greece) with low fertility and divorce rates and a few instances of cohabitation and births outside wedlock (Roussel, 1992). More recent statistics confirm this fertility trend of the North/South divide model.

Despite the fact that the European population is increasingly growing, there are more deaths recorded than births. This increase is mainly due to migration waves. The visible negative trend in fertility rates is particularly the reality of a number of southern European countries while northern European countries display signs of increase birth rates (Eurostat, 2018a). An ever-growing ageing population is also becoming a reality particularly in countries with low birth rate and a high rate of emigration of youths for work purposes in countries like Greece and Italy.

In view of peculiar distinctive characteristics of family relations in various southern European countries, there are some commonalities worth exploring with reference to Guerrero and Naldini's (1997) family model. This model portrays the southern European family as having inclinations for generations living together in one household. It also includes the relatively strong kinship ties, nuclear family-oriented setting and the high institutionalization of marriage.

The centrality of southern European family-oriented principles still retains high-intensity family and kinship networks in which relations between generations are seen in terms of obligation and a sense of community. Social networks are considered as a valuable asset in the South. The centrality of the community is regarded as a form of social capital which, as Robert Putman puts it, 'features of social organisation such as networks, norms, and social trust ... facilitate coordination and cooperation for mutual benefit' (Putnam, 1995:67). This social capital is beneficial for three elements – confidence, reciprocity and networks. In view of studies on social integration, the concept of social capital and civic engagement, principally as counter-discourse on the effects of neoliberal policies, has been given importance in academic literature in recent years (Ferragina and Arrigoni, 2017). Predominantly in a neoliberal climate with rising economic inequality, social capital is considered as an engine for social inclusion and a tool for civil engagement. These tie in with the need to cultivate connections through the close network of social relations. One consequence of this situation, particularly in small states, is a high tendency for nepotism. This is apparent in statistics in which it is typical for southern European youth to find employment through their family connections compared to northern European countries – 69 per cent of Greeks, 65 per cent of Italians, 61 per cent of Spaniards and 58 per cent of Portuguese said that they got a job with the help of their families (Mendras, 1997).

The small size of landmass and population in countries like Malta permit a situation where instead of distant personalities who one only knows through mass media, public figures in Malta are intimately known. They might be neighbours, friends, patrons people with whom one can develop, or at least envisage developing, personal relationships (Armstrong and Mitchell, 2011). This can easily result in a situation of clientelism. Clientelism is specifically typical in small societies. The smallness of the islands of Malta makes it more prone to patron–client linkage and particularities relationships especially between citizens and politicians (Boissevain, 1965, 1974). Clientelistic politics persist in Malta due to direct, face-to-face contacts between citizens and politicians and reciprocal relationship between patron and client; 'clientelistic practices and systems of patronage are what make Malta's political system functional' (Mitchell, 2002:43).

However, this sense of community often also heightens the status given to honour and shame which limits the degree of individuality and expression. Honour refers to the value in the eyes of the community. Similar to goodness and virtue in line with the collective conscience, honour runs parallel to compliance to traditional patterns of behaviour (Schneider, 1971). On the contrary, shame accentuates a state of no decency, modesty and losing or lacking respect for others in the community (O'Reilly Mizzi, 1994). The importance given to honour and shame is in itself a form of social control which regulates social behaviour. This kind of highly connected family network, with young people dependent on their parents till their late twenties and early thirties, can be at times smothering their sense of individuality and adventure (Sultana and Baldacchino, 1994); 'it could feel like growing up in a strait jacket of community surveillance, given the dense psycho-social atmosphere' (Sultana and Baldacchino, 1994:17).

Leaving parental home

Southern intergenerational relationships are essentially cushioning the effects of young people in transition to adulthood. Leaving parental home is in itself an important rite of passage. This does not always denote a complete transition to adulthood though, especially when young people still depend on parental financial support or return back to live with their parents after a period of independent living. For this reason, some even dubbed millennials as the 'boomerang' generation for their tendency to keep going back to their parental home after graduation (Newman, 1999). Culturally, young adults in the South still live with their family of origin after they finish their studies and enter the job market. They only leave parental home upon marriage and procreation. This is in part due to the high intensity of kinship networks (Guerrero and Naldini, 1997). This contrasts the situation in northern countries, in which young people go through a number of intermediate steps, such as living alone, cohabiting with a partner and a long period of married life without children. In EU countries, 28.5 per cent of young people aged between 25 and 34 were still living with their parents in 2016. Whereas in Nordic member states this rate is less than 10 per cent (Denmark 3.8 per cent, Finland 4.3 per cent, Sweden 6 per cent), in southern European countries the rate is much higher (Greece 55 per cent, Italy 48.9 per cent, Malta 51.5 per cent) (Eurostat, 2018c).

This degree of dependence of young people on their parents in southern European countries is often construed as both a burden and a valuable asset. These young people have an inclination to stay longer at their home of origin, many of them well into their thirties. There are various reasons for this economic dependency on parents. Yet it is equally important to refer to a number of cultural factors and their implications on the delay in leaving parental home.

First, it is a useful strategy to maximize grown children's resources under favourable conditions, including by lengthening the years in education, considered as a profitable personal investment.

Second, it is an undeniable fact that the time when to leave parental home is not necessarily decided independently by the individual as the result of free choice. Extended years in education, as well as the increase in short-term contracts jobs and high rate of unemployment, all have considerable impact on the transition of youth into independent living. Increased job competition has contributed to gradually prolonging transitions to financial independence (Bynner and Côté, 2008). Such financial situation is one of the main reasons why youth tend to delay leaving parental home.

Third, prolonging of partial dependence of youth is also the consequence of increase in house prices over recent decades. The ability to have an independent lifestyle at a young age in a separate dwelling became even harder to access in the twentieth-first century. A total of 44 per cent of young Europeans stated that they cannot afford to leave parental homes, whereas 28 per cent agreed that not enough affordable housing is available (Eurostat, 2009). Thus, living at the parental home enables young people to save money for purchasing their first home, at times with the financial help of their family members.

The delay in leaving parental home is one of the consequences of familialism within the southern European family model. The 'slow motion' in the advancement of gender relations is also worth outlining when discussing the southern family model.

Family responsibility and gendered roles

It cannot be denied that in the last few decades fundamental changes had occurred in women's lives in terms of gender relations, education, work, legislation and public life. With the shift from 'ascribed' to 'achieved' roles in contemporary Western societies, the female biography became increasingly individualized, to an extent that Beck and Beck-Gernsheim (1995) went as far as to suggest that 'men and women are released from the gender roles prescribed by industrial society for life in the nuclear family' (Beck and Beck-Gernsheim, 1995:5). The process of modernization is said to have progressively dissolved traditional family ties and disrupted normative sequences in life courses (Giddens, 1991, Beck, 1994, Bauman, 1996, Beck and Beck-Gernsheim, 2008[2002]). Just like the Becks (2008[2002]), it is fair to say that in recent years the female life biography underwent an individualization boost in the way they directed their energies towards establishing a career. Yet their assertion on a comprehensive liberation from traditional roles is not neatly applied in the southern European region.

The younger generation of women is adopting a new gender order and moving away from the traditional family model of rigid division of labour at home. Increase of flexibilization of employment practices in the contemporary Western societies for both men and women is presumably promoting a more family-friendly model and contributing to greater gender equity. Paid employment for women means that they are consolidating their position as paid workers and securing financial independence.

It is equally true that young women are progressively displaying expectations that extend beyond family obligations. A number of factors are contributing to this move towards greater gender equality. The improvement of women's education in the last few decades and the opening up of the educational system for women granted them greater access to higher education. This resulted in intergenerational mobility, having the average educational level of young women today higher than that of their parents, especially their mothers (Beck and Beck-Gernsheim, 2008[2002]).

Whereas in the 1980s, the proportion of young people in higher education was favourable to men in southern countries like Italy, Spain and Greece, in the last twenty years, there has been a substantial increase in the number of women in tertiary education in such countries, with more women as university students than men by the 1990s in universities in Portugal, Greece and Spain (Bonke, 1995). Yet, the situation is still far from being even-handed. When it comes to choices of university courses, statistics indicate that especially in the South, there is a tendency for a gender gap in the choice of courses. Girls tend to outnumber boys in general programmes; however, the opposite is said when analysing vocational programmes (Eurostat, 2009). In countries like Greece, Italy, Cyprus and Malta, less than 70 girls for every 100 boys were registered in vocational programmes (Eurostat, 2009). This feminization of courses is found in certain fields of education like humanities, arts and education.

The outcome of having better educational opportunities for girls is not only on a cognitive level but also in many aspects of their everyday life. One of the most obvious shifts in the life-course transitions of such females is the way that paid employment is no longer regarded as an intermediate phase until marriage.

Notwithstanding women's strides made towards obtaining professional careers and measures for equalization between the sexes in education and employment, it shouldn't be allowed to lull us into assuming an equitable situation. Gender inequality still prevails in most European countries and women still face barriers in pursuing real choices to achieve their full potential. It is worth addressing here structural issues, rather than individual challenges, that account for women lagging behind their male counterparts at work. EU documents, such as the 'Strategy for Equality between Women and Men 2010–2015' (European Commission, 2011), highlight the situation of inequality between women and men and propose ways how to increase equality. It reports that while the employment rate of women is increasing, it remains lower than that of men even though women represent a majority of students and university graduates. Furthermore, on average women earn 17.8 per cent less than men for every hour worked. Women still remain very much under-represented in economic and political decision-making positions (European Commission, 2011). This situation is particularly more problematic in southern Europe.

More often than not, women in the South are still endowed by the main responsibility of family life and childcare. They are still highly expected to perform their role to carry and nurture children – something that is still heavily contested by feminists as a condition influenced by normative cultural expectations rather than as 'natural' and biological. In southern European countries, women are more likely to assume care responsibilities at home and they are less likely to work outside the home, when compared with northern countries (Eurostat, 2019b).

Despite this, in recent years there has been a considerable increase in the number of women in the workforce. Yet, the influx of women in the labour market may not always signify more liberal gender-role ideologies but it is often the result of family strategies for collective income procurement. What's more, discourses by politicians on this increase are often surrounded on the need to have more individuals economically active for a sustainable welfare state – Women are more or less a 'reserve army of workers' to tame the instability in the economic situation of not having enough workers to provide for pensions in an ageing population.

Further to what I have maintained in 'Structure and Agency: Changes in Personal Agency in the Life Domain of Young Women in Malta' (Visanich, 2018), liberating conditions from normative roles created a contradictory situation especially for young females who are now faced with greater individual choice but they also have to shoulder more responsibilities. They are hardly considered completely released from traditional gender roles. Besides their reflexive deliberations, females in the South are very much aware of their struggles to juggle work and family. Albeit the rapid increase in the rate of working women, there is still a considerable division of gender roles, a noticeable glass-ceiling and a substantial gender pay gap in the South, in most cases scoring at the lowest scale amongst other European countries.

Historically, the Catholic Church and its all-male clergy along with the political structure were active agents working to inhibit female participation in the labour market in southern European countries. Take the situation of Malta as an example. It was a matter of fact that the baby boom generation was socialized into segregated gender duties which limited girls' opportunities for education and employment. The Church was constantly discouraging women's participation in the labour market, mainly through the use of mass media influencing public opinion into believing that 'woman's place is at home'. The Social Action Movement (a Catholic lay association) in the 1950s clearly demonized women who participated in the labour market by highlighting the detriment done to the family life:

> Married women should, as a rule, avoid all kinds of employment. The consequences of the employment of married women on married life may be generally classified as adverse effects, such as the refusal to bear children or neglect the children's education. (Social Action Movement, 1956:5–6)

Financial independence for women during this time was interpreted as resulting into difficulties of financial management when they reach their presumed 'ultimate' goal in life – Holy Matrimony (*Lehen is-Sewwa* [Voice of Truth] – newspaper of the Catholic Church, 1945).

Legislation in the twentieth century had also limited women's paid employment through the 'marriage bar', leading to widespread practices of denying jobs to married women. In Malta, for instance, women were discriminated by the 'marriage bar' up until December 1980:

> The marriage bar served as a constant reminder that, in the eyes of the State, the place of the married woman was not in the labour force, despite her talents, but in homemaking and nurturing. (Camilleri, 1997:27)

This was done to keep male unemployment low and enforcing in the process the role of women within the domain of domestic labour. Throughout the last sixty years, woman's employment rate increased gradually especially with the drive for industry plans to increase economic activity. Labour-intensive industries investing in Malta created job opportunities for many young women (Pollacco, 2003). However, at that time, the reactionary Catholic agenda was working to counteract such change with disseminating fear of the deterioration of the traditional family.

Various measures are currently in place in Malta to increase female participation in the labour market. These include the availability of free childcare centres for all working mothers, tax breaks for women returning to work after childbirth and the increase in promoting flexible and family-friendly working conditions.

Irrespective of these measures, Malta like other southern EU countries still scores quite low in EU statistics when it comes to rates of female employment compared to men and ranks high in gender pay-gap discrepancies. The difference in employment rate for men and women is at 11.5 in the EU average (EU28). In southern European countries, this gap is wider, predominantly in Malta (24.1 per cent), Italy (19.8 per cent) and Greece (19.7 per cent) (Eurostat, 2019b). Women are more involved in precarious sectors of the labour market; they are more likely to carry out temporary fixed-term work and be part of the informal economy. This is partly symptomatic of the way women decide to stay in casual or part-time work and choose not to further their career as a strategy to cope with doing the 'second shift' at home, that of caring for children and all the family members in general. More than fifteen years after the first publication of *The Second Shift*, Arlie Hochschild's (1990) work on women's disproportionate share of domestic and childcare responsibilities in dual-career households remains somewhat valid particularly when making sense of females' lives in the South.

In view of this, it is undoubtedly the case that despite the increased degree of agency in the lives of women in recent years, they are still not completely released from their gender roles as the Becks have asserted. When it comes to the labour market in southern Europe, women's position remains disproportionately different from their male counterparts, as evident in recent EU statistics which draw certain similarities in gendered work patterns in the South.

Conclusion

The family and welfare are relatively closely intertwined in southern European Mediterranean countries when compared to other welfare regimes. The presence of strong family ties acting as welfare provision is pivotal in policymaking in these countries, and they are often cushioning the effects of certain life crisis like unemployment and financial instability.

As explained throughout this chapter there are certain transversal cultural characteristics in the lives of families in the South. Traditionally, the typical attributes of the southern European family are very much based on the centrality of family-oriented principles, socially conservative norms and values, intragenerational solidarity and family obligations. This is deep rooted in communal practices and religious norms. It is quite common to have stress put on the institutionalization of marriage, whereas have a relatively low cohabitation, divorce rates, births outside wedlock and lone parent households. The chapter explored how the southern European family relations between generations are seen in terms of obligation, at times with different generations living together in one household. It also dealt with the low female employment in formal labour market and disproportionately gendered division of labour as one cultural condition in the South. The next chapter continues to understand these transversal particularities by focusing on one country in the South.

6

Slow motion changes in the South: The case of a small Southern European state

Lewis Carroll's fairy tale *Alice in Wonderland* is an impeccable antidote to the smallest southern European island state of Malta:

> *'I wish you wouldn't squeeze so,'* said the Dormouse, who was sitting next to her. *'I can hardly breathe.'*
> *'I can't help it'*, said Alice very meekly: *'I'm growing.'*
> *'You've no right to grow here'* said the Dormouse
> *'Don't talk nonsense'* said Alice more boldly: *'you know you're growing too.'*
> *'Yes, but I grow at a reasonable pace,'* said the Dormouse: *'not in that ridiculous fashion'* (Lewis Carroll, *Alice in Wonderland*)

Malta's pedal-on-accelerator economic growth, the highest rate in Europe, its pro-business mentality and its obsession with credit ratings are habitually interpreted in terms of the political tribal system of this small island state.

This chapter specifically focuses on one southern European country, the Maltese islands, to address the implications of cultural, historical and socio-economic conditions on its development which in return substantially shape the life experiences of young people. Despite the differences in economic realities of Malta with other southern European countries, Malta is referred to here as one exemplary case of how it has adapted, at a different speed to other southern countries, to broader European socio-economic systems. Compared to other Western locations, economic developments as well as the individualization process were 'delayed' in ex-colonial locations like Malta. Gaining its Independence from Britain in the mid-1960s meant that it experienced a period of job loss with the rundown of British and NATO military base. In view of such instability, it tended to be late in the processes of socio-economic and cultural changes compared to other Western European countries. Malta's economic development reached a surge in the last three decades of the twentieth century, with the development of the welfare state, the national health services and the implementation of subsidized housing.

The Maltese case

Malta is an archipelago of islands in the Mediterranean Sea occupying only 122 square miles and has a history starting approximately 5,000BC with the Neolithic and the first farming communities (Blouet, 1993). Its history of domination dates back to 2,300BC during the Bronze Age, and was followed by a series of occupations by the Cartagians, Romans, Byzantines, Arabs, Normans, Spanish, the Hospitaller Order of St. John, French and the British before being granted its Independence in 1964. Lying 93 km south of Sicily and around 300 km from the Tunisian and Libyan coasts, Malta has a marginal European position, often referred to as being in an 'ambivalent' European position (Mitchell, 2002).

The assumed north–south divide in Europe with different trajectories of economic and political developments (Tsatsanis, 2009) is an important consideration when locating Malta within a wider European context. Compared to other countries in the northern hemisphere of Europe, southern European states like Portugal, Spain, Italy, Greece and Malta often manifest socio-economic and political underdevelopment. Rhodes (1997) expanded on this assumption that these countries are considered as underdeveloped, both politically and economically and outside the mainstream of Western democratic societies, even though Italy had been a solid member of that camp since the late 1940s, and Portugal, Spain and Greece had all made transitions to democracy and experiences rapid economic development since the late 1970s (Rhodes, 1997). The 150-year history of British colonial rule and its position in the Mediterranean make Malta no exception.

It is often taken for granted that micro-states like Malta are easily absorbed into the larger global economy due to their vulnerabilities (Easterly and Kraay, 2000). Similar to other European micro-states, Malta is more exposed to exogenous shocks than larger states because of its vulnerability to external economic and political strategies and environmental shocks (Briguglio, 1995). Some of the common features found in small states are openness, insularity or 'enclaveness', resilience, weakness and dependence (Sutton and Payne, 1993). Moreover, Malta is not only a micro-state but also a micro island state, making it an added peripheral and insular small state.

Culturally, similar to other countries in southern Europe, Malta's value-system is in constant oscillation accommodating 'modern' with the 'traditional'. In Jon Mitchell's (2002) anthropological study in Malta, 'modernity' and 'traditional' are defined as follows:

> On the one hand, 'tradition' was associated with Catholic morality, a way of – particularly family – life based on it ....On the other hand, it was associated, particularly by younger Maltese, with a 'backward' and increasingly anachronistic orientation to the world, that bore the hallmarks of Church hegemony. Similarly, 'modernity' encompassed an inherent ambivalence. On the one hand, it was associated with education, material wealth and progress, but on the other hand with material excess and the erosion of 'traditional' morality. (Mitchell, 2002:16)

Malta's particularities are comparable with Emmanouil Tsatsanis's (2009) description on the pattern of late industrialization in southern European countries. Such pattern refers to a relative economic underdevelopment, persisting institutional weakness, paternalistic political networks, marked by the pervasiveness of informal-vertical political linkages and widespread cultural conservatism. Despite the small size of its landmass and the lack of natural resources, Malta in the second half of the twentieth century experienced a process of export-led industrialization. Yet, similar to other southern European countries, Malta experienced quite different process of industrialization compared to countries in Western Europe. There are various factors marking this difference in Malta's process of industrialization (Brincat, 2009).

First, industrialization in Malta was not accompanied by an 'Industrial Revolution' and most productive activities continued to be carried out by small labour-intensive family-owned businesses and sole traders. This feature coupled with the large agricultural sector was a significant characteristic which distinguished the south from the north of Europe (Tsatsanis, 2009).

Second, further evidence of how Malta's industrial process did not fit with the Western model is in the operation of state-owned industries. Industries such as the dockyard remained state-owned up till the late 2000s and thus the idea of private businesses running for profit on capitalist lines was rather absent (Brincat, 2009). Such industries produced a substantial blue-collar working class but not an industrial bourgeoisie. The income generated by the colonial 'military-industrial' establishment also served in a way to help the Catholic hierarchy to increase its wealth, mainly by renting its land as well as with the rise of property value resulting from urbanization.

Third, industrialization in Malta was in no way associated with the degree of secularization as in Western European countries. To this day, religion still occupies a privileged position in Maltese society despite recent cultural changes.

Malta's colonial and postcolonial status

Just like Britain, Malta's material destruction and human sufferance during the Second World War resulted in the need for an urgent reconstruction and contingent financial aid. The amount deemed necessary totalled to over 42 million pounds (Woods, 1946). The House of Commons however declared that the financial aid given for Malta's reconstruction would not exceed 31 million pounds, whilst excluding funds for economic development. The Maltese Labour Party in its 1947 electoral proposal favoured domestic social reforms similar to those proposed by the British Labour Prime Minister Clement Attlee (1945–51). This seemed possible because the Attlee's administration itself worked to guide colonial territories to responsible self-government within the commonwealth, with conditions that ensured that people receive both a fair standard of living and freedom from oppression (Ansprenger, 1989).

During the 1950s, the leader of the Malta Labour Party, Dominic Mintoff, favoured integration with the UK (Pollacco, 2003). Malta's 'British connection' was, by the majority of the Maltese population taken for granted mostly because they believed that Britain would never voluntarily give up the islands and Malta (Pirotta, 1991). In line with this, the plan for political and constitutional integration was seen as means to allow economic development, security and national pride. In the Malta Labour Party manifesto for 1955, the integration proposal was described as the gradual incorporation of Malta into the political, financial and social institutions of the British Isles (Malta Labour Party Election Manifesto, 1955). This would guarantee that Britain would work to raise the social status of the people of these Islands to heights recorded in Great Britain (Malta Labour Party Election Manifesto, 1955). The Interim Report submitted by Balogh and Seers (1955) to the Maltese Prime Minister Mintoff stated:

> Malta's development and stability would be automatically assisted under the 'development area' arrangements for dealing with economically backward areas within the United Kingdom, Maltese social expenditures would be raised with external help towards the United Kingdom standards, and a much more direct political channel would be provided for influencing Service expenditure. (Balogh and Seer, 1955:XXXIII)

It is worth noting the benefits for Britain and private businesses by this proposed integration. Balough's report shared a belief for the need of export-led diversification of the Maltese economy, by stressing that 'there is labour relatively cheaply available that is the only attraction of Malta' (Brincat, 2009:49). Between the years 1950 and 1955, Mintoff approved of Malta becoming a constituency of the Westminster Parliament based on grounds of having an economic equivalence with Britain. This could have meant that Maltese people, especially youth, would share the same advantageous life chances as Britons. During the integration negotiation in the 1955 Legislative Assembly, the British government agreed to offer Malta their own representation in the British House of Commons. Furthermore, Mintoff insisted that the Maltese, just like the British, should have to be guaranteed with full employment and a raise in the Maltese economic standards within twelve years to the same levels enjoyed in the UK. The *Times of London* of 2 December 1953 reported about the close ties between Britain and Malta if the plan for integration was implemented:

> Would be given a status comparable to that of the Isle of Man, which comes under the jurisdiction of the Home Office though making its own laws and raising its own taxes. (*Times of London*, 2 December 1953)

Yet despite this plan, the Maltese population was divided into two; the 'pro-Britishers' who supported this and those who refused this integration, including the Conservative Nationalist party and the Roman Catholic

Church who feared competition by Protestantism (Frendo, 1988:198). Consequently, although the referendum in February 1956 revealed a large support for integration, the Nationalist Party and the Church boycotted this decision.

What's more, the lack of agreement over the redundancy of naval dockyard workers made Mintoff abandon the plan for integration and instead supported independence outside the Commonwealth (Frendo, 1988). In December 1958, as part of his new plan for Malta, Mintoff stated:

> We would pledge ourselves never to make any military or other warlike alliance with any bloc or state. We would solemnly undertake to repair the merchant or naval shipping of any nation. As a denuclearized zone with a stable free society we would rapidly develop into a little Switzerland in the heart of the Mediterranean – a heaven of peace and rest for weary, disarmed tourists ... Given a stable outlet, American and European capital would flow into our parched land and the harmless industry of the West would serve without strings the rapidly expanding demands of the Arab countries. (Mintoff, 1959:101)

At the same time, however, George Borg Olivier, the leader of the Nationalist Party, was supporting Independence within the Commonwealth (Pollacco, 2003). Independence was finally granted on 21 September 1964.

The limit of political independence constituted various challenges in all postcolonial countries and Malta was no exception (Beeley and Charlton, 1994). Compared to other post-British colonial nation-states like Cyprus, and Singapore, the Independence of Malta was bequeathed with grievous social and economic problems. Gaining Independence meant giving power for political decision-making to the Maltese however this did not end the islanders' dependence on 'outsiders'. Malta's economic dependence on other countries for its development cannot be ignored.

Similar to other newly independent countries like Cyprus, Malta in the 1970s became a member of the Non-Aligned Movement, a group of nations made up of ex-colonies that did not form part of the 'developed' world. One of the purposes of such movement was to ensure sovereignty and the struggle against colonialism and imperialism. Both Malta and Cyprus ceased their membership in 2004 and joined the European Union (EU). Economic development in Malta, particularly in the last thirty years, coincided with the development of the welfare state, the national health services and the implementation of subsidized housing as well as universal benefits in healthcare and education.

The delay in economic development in postcolonial Malta, when compared to the situation of Britain during the 1960s, resulted in dissimilar life chances of youth in both countries. Whereas during the 1970s and 1980s the welfare state was being developed in Malta through the strengthening of national health services and the implementation of measures for subsidized housing, in Britain the reversal process was occurring with the implementation of a neoliberal agenda. While in the late 1970s Britain was experiencing a process of privatization, the Maltese state had control over banks, telecommunications, broadcasting, air and sea transport, and the dockyard. This suggests that Malta's socio-economic situation, as a postcolonial nation-state, hand in hand with its cultural characteristics resulted in the postponement (or even absence) of economic shifts taking place elsewhere in Western Europe. An example of this are the shifts within the educational system which happened at a slower pace compared to other countries in the West. An extensive historical overview is adequate here to outline this delay in the development of the educational system in Malta.

Historical overview on opportunities for higher education

Building on previous chapters in this book, there is no doubt that opportunities for higher education and employment opportunities are distinguishing factors with substantial implications on one's transitioning into adulthood. The lack of financial and human resources in Malta delayed the process to build an educational system based on meritocratic principles and accessibility for all. A report presented by Ellis in 1942 offered suggestions on measures needed to be implemented to (re)establish an adequate educational system in Malta (*Times of Malta*, 1943). The newspaper *Times of Malta* reported on Ellis's assessment, emphasizing the fact that 'the immediate and most pressing duty of the educational reformer is to provide for the children of the islands the best schooling possible under siege conditions' (*Times of Malta*, 1943:3).

Speaking on the situation of schooling during the post-war years, Ellis stressed the deficiencies in schools and the problem with lack of staff. Notwithstanding its limited resources however, the education system in Malta made a substantial leap forward between the years 1946 and 1971. Prior to 1946, parents had to pay fees to educate their children. With the introduction of compulsory education up to 14 years of age in 1946, parents with financial difficulties could apply for exemption from fees. Later in 1955, with the financial help from the British government, new schools were built and the Minister of Education introduced free education for all (Zammit Mangion, 1992). Morning classes at secondary schools, preparatory secondary schools, teacher training colleges and technical schools became free of charge. Despite the fact that these measures opened the doors for a meritocratic educational system irrespective of one's class background, the places offered for students to attend state-owned secondary schools were not meeting the demand. Only few students were chosen by means of an eleven-plus examination and given the opportunity for higher education.

During the post-war years, another obstacle in the Maltese educational system was the lack of training provision for teachers. This was addressed by designing teacher training courses attracting many young people in the 1960s. Between October 1948 and 1953, students attended a one-year residential training course, whilst plans were made to extend this to a two-year course. However, such change required a much larger building to accommodate both first- and second-year students attending this course. The Society of the Sacred Heart went ahead with the plan and the 'Mater Admirabilis Training College' for young women was opened by Queen Elizabeth II in 1954 (Department of Education, 1948/54). In a state of urgency to open a similar institution for young men, grants from the UK made possible the construction of St. Michael's Training College which opened in the same year. Furthermore, the Commonwealth Teacher Training Scheme in 1960 offered scholarships for academic and training courses in Britain to an average of twenty-three candidates every year (Department of Education, 1960).

Additionally, opportunities for tertiary education at the Royal University of Malta were scarce for young people. The University of Malta at that time, as a rule, only admitted fee-paying students (Galea, 2003). Only a few hundred new candidates entered the University per year between the 1950s and 1970. The total majority of these students were males. In 1960, only nineteen female students (8 per cent) attended the Royal University of Malta. This number rose to 109 female students (19 per cent) in 1965 and up to 165 (21 per cent) by 1970 (Nicolas, 1974). It was only in 1971 that Maltese students were exempted from paying tuition fees to follow a course at university (Cassar, 2009).

For those youth who did not want to or couldn't follow a university course but instead opted for having training in vocational courses, opportunities were equally limited in the 1960s. Addressing this problem, the then Minister of Education Agatha Barbara claimed that technical education '[had] been suffering from a confused and deficient structure. We never had any serious training in the trades' (Legislative Assembly Debates, 1972). With the help of Italian grants, tools and equipment were donated to local trade schools (Zammit Mangion, 1992). Apart from the opening of Trade Schools for boys over fourteen years of age, a similar school was opened for girls, specializing in trades of dress-cutting, industrial sewing, needlework, crochet and toy-making (Sultana, 1992). The specialization of these schools manifested clearly the division of labour based on gender differences.

In the last forty years, various measures were in place aimed at the extension and expansion of the educational system in Malta. These include having free post-compulsory education and handing out universal maintenance grants to student to encourage further education. Maltese citizens who are currently studying at the University of Malta do not pay fees for their undergraduate studies and are provided with a universal maintenance grants and a stipend during their course of studies; a measure that aimed at increasing access to tertiary education for all. However, this initiative is not completely reaching its objectives because the number of Maltese youth with tertiary education attainment (30 per cent) is lower than the EU average (39.9 per cent) (European Commission, 2018). Another challenge in the current Maltese educational system is the high early school leaving rate (20.3 per cent) aged between eighteen and twenty-four years which is considerably higher than the EU average of 10.6 per cent (European Commission, 2018).

Economic shifts in recent years

Similar to other states in Europe, Malta's post-war unstable economic situation had a severe impact on one's lived experiences especially due to high level of unemployment. To address economic challenges in the 1960s, the government of the day designed strategies to overcome such difficulties. The first Development Plan, published in 1959, aimed at counteracting unemployment by creating 7,500 new jobs (Jones, 1971). This plan was based on measures for economic diversification, mainly by promoting manufacture, tourism and, to a much smaller extent, agriculture (Department of Information, 1959). However, by 1964, only 1,800 new employments were created. This modest rate of progress did not in any way compensate for the high number of redundancies resulting from the British Forces rundown in 1962 and throughout the following years. In the post-war years, 30 per cent of the population was either directly employed by the British forces or in industries serving the military machine (Pollacco, 2003).

By 1964, the number of unemployed increased almost ninefold since 1946 and amounted to 8 per cent of the total workforce, mainly because HM servicemen had decreased its workforce by 45.5 per cent (Pollacco, 2003). A number of 14,700 workers lost their jobs with the HM Services department between the years 1958 and 1969 (Pollacco, 2003) In light of these shifts, being young in the 1960s in Malta meant living at times of rising unemployment, heavy emigration and fears for the future of the newly Independent country.

The second Development Plan for the 1964–1969 period aimed to target these economic realities and thus preventing the lowering standards of living. The government of the day was faced with the task of creating an economy from scratch, with no natural resources to fall back upon. Efforts were made to diversify the economy primarily with the growth of the tourism industry, which to this day remains one of the main pillars of the Maltese economy (25 per cent of GDP), and in more recent years the expansion of financial services and the IT sector.

During times of economic crisis and the high rates of unemployment, emigration was considered as a safety-valve. In an attempt to stabilize the standards of living, an annual average net emigration of 7,500 people was aimed over a five-year plan between the years 1959 and 1964 (Jones, 1971).

Emigration was deemed as inevitable and indispensable to avoid widespread unemployment and the lowering of the standards of living (Cachia Zammit, 1963). The Maltese peak of emigration in the mid-1960s was very much a reflection of the economic fluctuation in Malta coupled with economic expansion in the respective destination countries. In the same manner, the downward curve in the number of migration witnessed after 1974 reflected rising unemployment and economic fluctuations in the destination countries. Maltese migration patterns to Australia, the UK and North America were partly due to the common bond of the English language. There are also certain similarities with Cyprus, and other small island communities, such as the Azores and the Aeolian Island, whose migrants habitually moved to longer distances such as the United States and Australia, probably because of the seafaring tradition of small island communities (King, 1979).

The Labour government of the day in Malta embarked on an ambitious development plan of nationalization with the intention to promote economic growth and social reform as well as to lesser British influence in the country. In an attempt to attract foreign investment in Malta to remain competitive, wage increases were low in the 1970s.

Throughout the years, the Maltese economy stabilized and the rate of unemployment gradually decreased. In contemporary Maltese society, the rate of unemployment (3.5 per cent) is amongst the lowest in all the member states as opposed to other southern European countries (Greece 18.1 per cent, Spain 13.6 per cent and Italy 9.9 per cent) and the EU average of 6.3 per cent (Eurostat, 2019d). When it comes to youth unemployment, the situation is equally favourable in Malta (10.3 per cent) compared to the EU average rate of 14.3 per cent and other southern European countries like Greece (40.4 per cent), Spain (31.7 per cent) and Italy (30.5 per cent) (Eurostat, 2019d). The European Economic Forecast (2016) reports that Malta's continued economic growth is based on strong labour market rudiments, including its robust job creation and low unemployment. The recent booming economic conditions may be considered as smoothening the transition from education to work for young people.

Albeit common cultural conditions with other southern European countries which were explored in the previous chapter, it is pertinent to address the disparate economic conditions of such countries. For example, Malta has not undergone an economic crisis as experienced in countries like Greece, Italy, Spain and Cyprus. On contrary, the GDP growth rate in Malta averaged at 0.94 per cent between 2000 and 2018 (Trading Economics, 2019). At present times, Malta is enjoying a rate of full employment of all graduates at the rate of 94.5 per cent compared to the EU average of 80.2 per cent (European Commission, 2018).

Application of laissez-faire measures and individualization

As I have stressed in previous chapters, the individualization thesis rests on a number of premises, mainly detraditionalization, disembedding institutionalization, compulsory pursuit of 'a life of one's own' and the intensification of risks of the individual due to precarious freedoms. The process of individualization in the Anglo-American context and the Western society at large is said to have intensified in the everyday life of individuals in tandem with the spread of subjective neoliberalism as a hegemonic mode of doing things.

Not surprisingly, the emergence of the 'spirit' of individualization in Malta intersected with socio-economic changes. In particular, neoliberal practices are increasingly apparent in the last decade, in spite of pressures from the Catholic Church, as the main supporting pillar in society, to continuously work for the promotion of a collective conscience – the antithesis of neoliberalism. An all-pervasive neoliberal mentality is currently present on various fronts in the Maltese society, specifically within the increased stress put on having a market-oriented mentality – a mentality that puts pressure on the 'good' derived from business as a condition of late modernity, as Jim McGuigan (2005) has argued. An example of this neoliberal mentality is the mindset on the growth of the construction industry, pedalled by insatiably greedy contractors who are currently defacing the Maltese landscape. Short-sighted politicians emphasize the benefits to continue to pedal on to this system for pursuit of job creation and economic growth. The capital city of Valletta is a case in point of the application of this neoliberal mentality in its recent gentrification process, partly as an effort to showcase it as it hosted the title the European Cultural

Capital in 2018. Valletta, just like some other cities of Capital of Culture, is an exemplary case for the efficacy of culture-led regeneration and neoliberal development. Success for hosting the title is measured in terms of competitiveness, increase in business and regeneration.

Trying to make sense of this during a public meeting on the impact of the gentrification of the city for research purposes, one resident polemically expressed this neoliberal mentality:

> There's a feeling that financial well-being is the only form of well-being, there is no pursuit of beauty or spirituality, but we need to look beyond this amazing economic growth to which we have all submitted. (Hudson, 2019, *Maltatoday* online)

Specifically, during the last two decades, the spread of neoliberalism in manufacturing is apparent with companies in Malta experiencing a fair share of relocation to cheaper labour costs elsewhere, or were threatened to do so. Most of the time, the government of the day adopted laissez-faire policies and seemed powerless to halt this trend (Debono and Farrugia, 2008). Such policies often resulted in a threat of massive redundancies of employees particularly within the textile industry in Malta. A case in point is within the Denim services, where around 1,200 employees faced redundancy. Due to the smallness of the Maltese labour market, the closing down of one major company could result in huge strains on the economy. Thus, with the threat of a sudden upward curve in unemployment rates, the need for collective bargaining was inevitable. Another case in point is the company ST Electronics, one of the largest semiconductor suppliers in Europe, which in 2006 planned 3,000 layoffs from its European branches including from the Maltese branch (Debono and Farrugia, 2008). With the union's persuasion for collective bargaining, an agreement was eventually reached to shield Maltese workers, mostly young people, from redundancy. In another similar situation, the union intervened to avoid dismissal in one of the leading clothing manufacturers, Bortex, when parts of its production were transferred to Tunisia, Bulgaria and China to cut labour costs.

In order not to have any job loss in the Maltese factory, the union agreed to a wage freeze and for the company to postpone the renewing of the company collective agreement. Recent measures taken to counteract this situation are that instead of competing for cheap labour costs within the low-end high-volume market other niche markets are being considered as a more viable option. Such examples are foreign direct investment in high value-added sectors such as pharmaceuticals and IT (Debono and Farrugia, 2008).

These instances are clear examples of how global neoliberal processes have significant impact on the local labour market. This is felt not only by the relocation of companies but also in privatization of various entities such as Maltacom (state telecommunication company), Seamalta (state shipping company) and the Malta International Airport.

The spread of neoliberalism and individualization: Inhibiting cultural agents

Whereas the aforementioned structural economic conditions are key factors in the spread of neoliberalism, cultural settings that enable or inhibit it, cannot be left unnoticed. In order to take stock of this, I am here outlining two of the cultural agents in Malta which limit the spread of neoliberalism due to their emphasis on collective orientation. These are the Catholic religion and the family kinship network. Intentionally, I am referring to the same cultural indicators identified in previous chapters making part of the southern European commonalities. The scope of doing this is to make sense of how these enable or prohibit the process of neoliberalism in the Maltese society.

First, similar to other countries in the south, Catholicism in Malta occupies a privileged position that is likely to generate consent over the masses. The close relationship of the Church and the state often transmits the perception that the Maltese state represents an entirely Catholic population, whilst allowing no space to other forms of religious practices (Frendo, 1988). Catholicism in Malta often equates to nation-state identity and occupies a privileged position generating consent over the masses; often seen as instrumental in promoting good citizenship and social conscience as against a more individualized lifestyle. The Maltese historian Henry Frendo (1988) addressed the importance and presence of the Church in Malta when saying:

The parochial structure was intact: religion was at the heart of Maltese lie just as the church was physically in the centre of the village, and formed part of the strong social nexus by which the common people looked up differentially to the 'respectable' members of the community. (Frendo, 1988:188)

What's more, Catholicism in Malta is considered to place Malta at the margin of Europe, both inside and outside European 'modernity'. Catholicism was a means of legitimizing the accession to Europe, however, it was also a tool for resisting it (Mitchell, 2002).

Where younger men and – particularly – women were adopting or attempting to adopt more 'modern', 'European' lifestyles, their parents and grandparents saw this as the beginning of the end for Maltese morality. Younger people were more ambivalent. (Mitchell, 2002:71)

In view of this, Malta was referred to as 'neo-traditional', very similar to Cyprus in terms of the modern/tradition dichotomy set against the European model of development (Abela, 1991, Argyrou, 1996); traditional because it still has a Catholic morality, but 'neo' due to its incorporation of a modernist orientation to the economy and rationality. Vassos Argyrou (1996) studied such characteristics of 'tradition' and 'modernity' in Cyprus in order to analyse the extent to which Cypriot culture is becoming subject to Western hegemony. His anthropological study framed this analysis by focusing on Greek Cypriot weddings, as a symbolic struggle between traditional identity and the more Westernized outlook to life. By acknowledging the 'backwardness' of this culture, Argyrou (1996) also emphasized the modernizing trends that place Cyprus in a continuous struggle for symbolic domination. Despite that Abela's (1991) and Argyrou's (1996) studies are rather dated, yet they are still somewhat relevant to an extent.

Another factor influencing the impact of individualization in Malta is family kinship ties, counteracting individualized inclinations. As explored systematically in the previous chapter, the typical form of intergenerational relation is prominent in the southern region. The Maltese family retained many of the traits of the southern European family model, as pinpointed by Guerrero and Naldini (1997). Boissevain (2006) addressed the importance of the Maltese family as an institution with an all-embracing wide network of blood relatives:

> Not only is the family the basic unit of Maltese society, it is also the basic unit of the Catholic Church, which [...] plays an extremely important part in Maltese social life. The Church regards the family as the principal unit of religious socialisation. In the family the individual first learns the values and mission of the Church into which he is born. The family is also the primary unit of reproduction for the Church, the agency through which it replaces and increases its numbers. (Boissevain, 2006:17)

In spite of these peculiarities one cannot ignore the recent changes in Malta which indicate a more liberal society, often interpreted in terms of the weakening ties with the Church influencing everyday life. The increase in immigration flows, in recent years, is contributing further to the growing numbers of intercultural marriages, and increasing Westernized trends of diversification in family life, not solely based on the traditional model.

Yet still, both marriage and separation rates fit well within the southern European family model, characterized by a family culture where marriage rate remains high and is very much under the influence of the Catholic Church. In the Latin family of nations such as Portugal, Italy and Spain, divorce law was introduced very late in the process compared to other Western countries. This is a clear case of how southern European countries adopted glocally to Western tendencies. Instead of having a universally cultural development that suggests global uniform trends, the process of glocalization addresses the increasing diversification and the importance of the particularities of the location that make up one's dispositions.

In the non-Latin Catholic country of Ireland, divorce was introduced in the 1990s. As for Malta, the legalization of divorce was delayed further and only became legalized recently in 2011, following a national referendum. The organization of civil society has been significant in establishing a number of campaigns promoting civil activism particularly within the 'Yes' movement for the legislation of divorce; a movement which led to a victorious referendum and subsequently the legislation of divorce in 2011. Even though the majority of the Maltese voted in favour of divorce legislation, the anti-divorce campaign, orchestrated by the Church, was in its full force using its means to transmit the traditional Catholic values.

In recent years, an equally important social movement promoting a liberal society was the gay rights movements which pushed forward the legislation of same-sex unions, resulting in the enactment of Civil Union Act in 2014. In less than a decade, various legislative changes on social and sexual rights were in place; consequentially putting Malta as the first European country to ban 'gay conversion therapy'. Yet paradoxically, albeit discourses on social rights and an increase in feminist movements, abortion is still illegal in Malta. Grounded in moral arguments, the legalization of abortion is still under discussion, with a handful of in-favour movements debating its introduction, yet having members of parliament and the Church strongly opposing this legislation. It comes to no surprise that in his first clear statement, the newly sworn-in President of Malta Dr George Vella in April 2019 stated that he will not sign the abortion legislation and that this should remain illegal with no exception.

Conclusion

Indisputably, there is a clear disparity between different locations as to how far the individualization process has advanced in line with their political history, the 'delay' in economic changes and the spread of neoliberalism. The Maltese case, as one of the smallest countries in southern Europe, is a typical example of some of the shared economic and cultural setting in this region. On the European map, Malta shares with its neighbouring southern European countries a 'slow motion' in economic development. Additionally, cultural conditions, including the continuous relevance of family-oriented principles and the religious institution counteracting individualized inclinations, are equally important to address. These have significant implications on the advancement of the individualization process and the spread of neoliberalism on an economic level as well as a subjective mode of attribution. The next chapter explores this further by referring to the actual meanings of a small sample of millennials in Malta in an attempt to make sense of the workings of these societal conditions in the south in everyday experiences.

7

The meanings and feelings of tertiary-educated millennials in the South

> Our life revolves around the fact that we go to university, find a job, find a partner and get married. But I believe that there is so much more to that. From the comments I receive from my parents I realize that I am not normal ... My father always asks me whether I had found the one ....I want to travel and find a job which allows me to travel. (Sandra, postgraduate student in Marketing)

Life trajectories of millennials, as defined by Sandra, pose important questions about the process of negotiating strategies to accommodate normative aptitudes with personal agency. This chapter develops further on the social, historical, economic and cultural conditions, as examined in the previous chapter, by focusing on a more micro approach. It draws on from some of the outcomes of a qualitative study I conducted on the life situations of tertiary-educated millennials in Malta. Survey data on education and employment opportunities amongst youth are valuable to provide a snapshot of the actual situation yet they pose limitations in explaining the real meanings and feelings of youth. The research I refer to in this chapter attempts to fill this gap by providing knowledge on the meanings of a small number of Maltese millennials who have had opportunities for tertiary education. Qualitative citations were selected for this chapter to reflect typical patterns of responses. The majority of them were transitioning from full-time education to their first full-time jobs during the time of the interview between the years 2010 and 2012. Others were doing their postgraduate degrees to equip themselves better before entering the labour market. I had recently followed these participants, who are now in their thirties, to have an update of their life situation. They were all in full-time jobs, still living in Malta, earning above average income and were financially independent and have left their parental home. Out of all participants only three remained unmarried and without having children.

The twelve ethnographic interviews and a focus group, based on acquiring contact and interaction with participants to make sense of what the world is like for them, were conducted over a period of approximately twenty-four months. Clearly, such sample size is insufficient to argue on generalized attitudes of youth with tertiary education in the south. However, it does give an indication on the meanings and feelings of some of these youths, particularly on their strategies of negotiation and accommodation of cultural circumstances with their individualized lifestyle. My primary concern in this chapter is to elicit relevant knowledge from the research related to the notions of agency, the degree of anxiety and how this is cushioned by cultural peculiarities.

This chapter discusses the notion of 'compromised choices' which refers to youths' attempt to strike a balance between their willingness to gratify cultural norms and their desires to design their own life plan. This notion builds on the concept of 'structured individualization' (Nagel and Wallace, 1997, Rudd and Evans, 1998, Furlong and Cartmel, 2007[1997], Côté, 2010) as a balanced view of the structure–agency relation in the life experiences of youths. Both reflexive deliberations and the role of the social context on dispositions are given equal importance in making sense of actions (Elder-Vass, 2007).

Fieldwork

Primarily, it is useful to sketch out the fieldwork process of this research which had weighty effects on the actual findings. The elicitation of knowledge went beyond a formal one-time interview process. I found that this does not always work well with young people who might feel uncomfortable knowing they are studied academically. On contrary, it felt necessary to obtain a 'thick description' as Geertz (1973) famously puts it, by conducting ethnographic interviews. This research tool goes beyond the spontaneous exchange of views in the form of a conversation, but focused on developing a collaborative relationship with participants and spending substantial amount of time, on a number of occasions, to careful question and listen with the intention to better understand their life situation. The aforementioned relationship was important in order to gain trust.

All participants whose interviews I am drawing here were white, heterosexuals and living in Malta. They all had tertiary education therefore their interpretations are by no means a normalized experience for all young people of the same age group. All ethical procedures were followed and participants recruited were informed on their rights to view transcripts, their right to withdraw from the research at any stage of the research process and to have their names changed to safeguard their anonymity.

Participants were briefed about the scope of the study and the reason why their participation was needed. They were also asked permission to record conversations and to use ethically the information they provided. The language used during my interviews was not simply a 'transparent carrier of facts, but as integral to the making of meaning' (Lawler, 2008:36). Interviews were transcribed not only word by word from oral to written language, but emphasis on intonation and emotional expressions were also included in the transcript. Even the use of language is considered crucial here, having in mind, the use of both Maltese and English languages as official languages in Malta.

In order to record details and events, a journal was kept that documented every encounter with participants. I met research participants on various occasions, many a time for a conversation over coffee. Just as Ken Pryce (1979) found himself going to clubs at night to become familiar with research subjects, I met participants on various occasions, with their consent, following them in their leisure activities. In some occasions I also attended events that participants were involved in. For instance, Mona, one of my research participant who is a young green activist invited me on various occasions to events, most of the time protests on environmental destruction. As for Sandra, I often met her in bars for sessions of beer drinking because it was her choice of how to wind down. Thus, rather than treating research participants as passive respondents, they were active collaborators in this study. In a similar way to how Ann Oakley (1981) regarded her participants in her research, participants became so involved in the research that they contacted me after the interviews to give me more information.

Yet, my own presence and reflexivity in this research warrants a thorough understanding because it played a weighty role during fieldwork. Researchers had long regarded reflexivity as part of the 'scientific method' with the aim to protect objectivity, validity and generalizability of the research (Johnson and Duberley, 2003:1293). Knowledge produced is considered as 'constructed' (Latour, 1987, Bourdieu and Wacquant, 1992). Knowledge is 'not something that people possess in their heads, but rather, something that people do together' (Gergen, 1991:270). No knowledge is ever strictly transparent and neutral for Latour (1987). Nevertheless, this viewpoint is too narrow for most scholars as they cast their doubts on whether researchers can 'with objectivity, clarity, and precision report on their own observations of the social world' (Denzin and Lincoln, 1994:11–12). An alternative to objectivity is the importance put on the social position of the researcher and the awareness of power relations throughout the fieldwork (Harding, 1986, Haraway, 1988, Denzin and Lincoln, 1994). The researchers' interpretation of the social world is embedded in the world of language, ideas and social relationships. Indeed, this process is inescapable from the very fact of our own 'being in the world' (Heidegger, 1992) and thus, interpretation-free, apolitical and theory-neutral facts are simply not possible (Alvesson and Skolberg, 2000:9).

Youths' situatedness of time and place and the impact of the cultural and economic situation influenced significantly their reflexive stance. It therefore made sense that this study involved the consciousness of social contingencies influencing the knowledge produced by participants, often generating a limited version of 'truth' (Haraway, 1988).

Social types of individual life biographies

The collaborative relationship with participants during ethnographic interviews allowed me to be able to draw a caricature of their particular social type, to illustratively have an image of the person being studied – similar to what Simmel (1950) regarded as a cast for the specifiable reactions and expectations of others which shape a typical orientation to the world. By the term 'social type', I am referring to the way an individual is recognized as a typical kind of a social category or social group and how this individual reminds us of others with similar values, behaviour, style and habits (Almog, 1998). Although informal, social types tend to become well conceptualized and belong to any particular kind of person who characteristically plays them. Social types are:

> consensual concepts of roles that have not been fully codified and rationalised, which help us find our way about in the social system .... they are a chart to role structure otherwise largely invisible and submerged. (Klapp, 1958:674)

Mona exemplified a 'boho' vegan social type and as an environmentalist with a strong determination to fight injustice and protest against animal cruelty. I met Mona at an annual World Fest event, an event selling fair trade products and promoting tribal and ethnic cultures. She embraced the notion of inner spirituality, adapted by East philosophies and prioritized going to India in the next couple of years. In her rather romanticized vision of the East, she maintained that she is attracted to Eastern philosophies because unlike the West, they focus on one's spiritual well-being instead of the zeal for money-making. She expressed her anti-consumerist ideology by refusing to wear or buy any form of globally branded products. As an avid fan of Naomi Klein's books, she strongly believed that the West is corrupted not only by greedy multi-national corporations but by the neoliberal ideology that infiltrated the hearts and minds of her peers. She described herself as 'ambitious, energetic, environmentalist and a bit existentialist sometimes'. She told me that 'where there is a quest for social justice, I tend to be involved'. Indeed, she strived very hard to live up to her ideals. I followed Mona around to some of the events she was co-organizing with others to fight for social injustices such as in the debate on 'Freedom for Palestine, Boycott Israel' and the march against censorship in Malta. Her verve to live up to her ideals to 'change the world' was very striking and not very much consistent in other discussions with young people.

Degree of agency

Similar to what Beck and Beck-Gernsheim (2008[2002]) argued on individualized biographies, the notion of agency was accentuated by the majority of participants. Fieldwork participants referred to their compulsion to orchestrate their lives on their own, as an important marker of entering adulthood. With incessant choices on what roles to enter, participants found it hard to distinguish the events bridging adolescence and adulthood. They felt at the crossroads somewhere between youth and adulthood. Just like Bauman's (1996) explanation of youths' experiences in postmodernity, they were more like 'tourists' rather than 'pilgrims'; sharing clear awareness of their goal, yet they were more interested in acquiring new experiences before reaching such goal.

Tying in with Beck and Beck-Gernsheim's argument, it was predominantly the case that most participants perceived their 'own life ... [as] no longer sedentary or tied to a particular place' (Beck and Beck-Gernsheim, 2008[2002]):180). Young people in this study referred to their customary activity of travelling for study or leisure purposes. Millennials have the advantage of not having their experiences limited to one location but they live a transnational life stretching across frontiers; what Beck and Beck-Gernsheim (2008[2002]) call the 'globalisation of life biographies'.

Andre went as far as to say that his priority was to travel around the world. He worked part-time jobs and saved money simply to travel. His thirst for acquiring new experiences and immerse himself in different cultures was his main motivation to get through university life and drag himself to graduate. In spite of this, he still acknowledged his eventual career goal, that of becoming a web designer:

> My priority is to travel around Europe and Australia. So I am planning to spend the next five years travelling. As soon as I graduate I will not start working immediately, I will travel instead. Ten years are too far off but I hope I will be settled by then. For instance, I wish to start my own business on web design. I wish to have a job which allows me to travel.

The strongest indicator of agency was in the participants' set priorities, to experience autonomous living and travel before 'settling down'. In one of the group conversations with Mark, Jane and David about life course transitions, they all referred to the individual ethic of self-fulfilment and achievement as their top priority in their present situations. Being in their twenties at the time of the interview, they felt they were too young to commit themselves to a lifelong relationship which brings with it certain individual limitations.

Sandra principally elucidated on this notion of agency. She was planning to do voluntarily work abroad for a short period of time. In spite of her rather conservative family background, as she described it, she detested normative transitions into adulthood but emancipated living on her own and making her own decisions. She maintained that the rigidity of normative life course stages limited an individual to 'just go through life'; instead she consciously wanted to devise her own life away from such normative model. Even though her full-time work provided her with financial security, it was not self-fulfilling and she felt tied down to the routine. She maintained that she wanted to quit her job and do voluntary work abroad, irrespective of her parents' insistence to 'settle down':

> I have friends my age who are getting married at twenty-two, twenty-three ... they seem happy, they seem in love, but for me it's foolishness, nothing else. I'm not saying it can't work, because it can work when there is real love, but there are so much things I want to do in life, that I'm sure that if I will have a partner I simply can't do them.

All participants interviewed shared common urges; to have a career and to travel around the world before 'settling down' in a marriage relationship. Possibly due to the insularity emanating from the smallness of the Maltese Islands, participants expressed their feelings of 'lack of space' and the need to travel as an uppermost priority. Naomi Klein (2009[2000]) fittingly described this feeling of lack of space by saying that young people feel like 'in Alex Garland's novel *The Beach*, looking for the one corner of the globe uncharted by the Lonely Planet to start your own private utopia' (Klein, 2005:64). The quest for time-out from the everyday so-called cut-throat life is felt by most participants I spoke to who were very keen on their travel escapes.

Nonetheless living abroad is mostly considered as a temporary phase for Maltese youth. According to local statistics, the majority (79.2 per cent) of youth within the age group 25–34-year-old saw themselves settling in Malta in their adulthood and were not willing to change their place of residence for a job (NSO, 2018).

Most participants referred to having a career and becoming financially stable as a step towards adulthood. In line with Arnett's (2004) argument, it was evident that young people were self-defining their adult identities on the basis of psychological factors like accepting responsibility for their own actions as well as making informed independent decisions. A case in point was Mark, who regarded adulthood as a stage when individuals become responsible for their own actions:

> I think when I started working at eighteen it was a step towards becoming an adult. It's a stage where you become responsible for yourself and your own actions. It also allows you to have your own money and decide for yourself what to do with it.

What was noticeable was that Mark regarded the feeling of preoccupation about the future as part of the process of becoming an adult: 'The future is a terminology that adults use. I still feel young to think about the future and prefer living day by day.' Most of the young people felt lost somewhere between youth and adulthood.

Most participants believed that one important step towards adulthood responsibility was their decision on which academic courses to choose; a decision which caused anxiety because its consequences are burdened on the individual:

> The difference is that now you have to take your own decisions compared to previous years. Till 16, my mum used to take most of my decisions but now I have to take some myself, for instance when it comes to university stuff, my mother can't help me. I have to take my own decisions now. (David, 22 years old)

The degree of anxiety

The primary contributing feature for anxiety, according to participants, had more to do with their feeling of uncertainty in choosing their career paths rather than the fear of unemployment itself. Their confidence in finding employment had to do partly with the low youth unemployment rates in Malta and the total employment of graduates.

In spite of the fact that participants emphasized that they deliberately chose which career to pursue, they were aware that the process that offered such choices also caused risks and consequentially apprehension. Just like in Beck and Beck-Gernsheim (2008[2002]) account, they felt that it was a matter of 'your own life – your own failure'. They felt pressured by the educational system to obtain higher educational qualifications with the hope of gaining an advantage in access to better-paying jobs.

Jane, a 24-year-old participant, said that she felt the need to increase her marketability by studying for a Master's degree. Equally worried about the lack of predictability, Maria, a 21-year-old participant, maintained that 'I am really anxious about my future. The fact that I won't have things planned out really scares me.' However, this apprehension about the future is not a new-fangled condition experienced for the first time by millennials. As mentioned in previous chapters, psychological and biological changes that young people go through are an integral aspect of the transition into adulthood, which all contribute to feelings of apprehension.

Nonetheless most of these participants with tertiary education maintained that underpinning these anxieties was the concern on the increase weight put on credentials. They were very much aware of the increased stress placed on qualifications. Obtaining a university degree became a universal goal for young people with their similar life chances. For them, a university degree was part of their trajectory into adulthood even though they were unsure what to do in their life. Lara's comment typified the taken for granted move to tertiary education after obtaining their Advanced levels:

> I am studying but I don't know for what. It was just a normal process that I had entered university after obtaining my Advanced Levels. But still, I don't know what I want to do in life and which job to go for.

Additionally, Jane reflected on this notion of furthering education by referring to intergenerational shifts. She felt she had more choices on which career to pursue compared to her parent generation. Her ambition was to be a psychologist. Regardless of Jane's perceived advantageous position for having the ability to devise her own life-plan, she also felt uneasy about her future and saw herself in a liminal stage as an 'emerging adult'. In a powerful discourse about the shift in females' life chances, Jane compared her situation with her grandmother's while remembering the way her grandmother narrated her past. She admitted that she had more things to think about, more stress to deal with and more uncertainty about what to do.

> Life was simpler. Although I think today women have more opportunities but I think life was simpler. Women had fewer anxieties. They only thought about marriage. So advancement has also brought about negative consequences like anxiety. A woman used to think about marriage and childcare whereas today she needs to balance the family with a career. Sometimes when I'm very anxious, by the way I'm a feminist, but sometimes I say it was better when we were simpler.

In view of this, her interpretation of her grandmother's narratives has to be viewed in terms of the construction and refraction of memory. The very fact that her grandmother was recalling on her past in retrospect, with knowledge on the events that followed as well as with feelings on the eroding of time-honoured stabilities, her interpretations of her nostalgic past were distorted. The notion of nostalgia is not only ingrained in the concept of the irreversibility of time and the lack of ability to transport back in the moment, but it has to do with the way the past actively engages with the present and future (Keightley and Pickering, 2006, Keightley, 2008). Equally important, it cannot be ignored that imagination and memory can never be represented in a transparent manner. Both imagination and memories are reconstructed and communicated in a narrative form which, to an extent, can be seen that 'all memories [and imagination] are representation[s]' (Terdiman, 1993:8) of the individual's subjectivity. Memory of an event modifies itself in relation to the person's reflections and understanding of that particular event. 'Truth', thus, depends on the genre of the story and its audience (Tonkin,1992).

Contrary to this situation, Jane was looking at her future aspirations with anxiety because she lacked the certainty of how things would turn out. Her 'do-it yourself biography', albeit exciting, was equally apprehensive especially when knowing that she had to prolong years in education before entering into full-time employment and become financially independent. Her decision to further her studies had also a substantial impact on how much leisure time she had at her disposal. The concept of work–life balance and the support structures in place, particularly in southern European countries, including the hands-on involvement of close family members, warrants careful examination when studying time and financial management for youth.

Negotiation and accommodation of cultural conditions

Indisputably, values placed on the family and sexuality in Maltese society had shifted in the last few decades. Most research participants expressed a secular and rational viewpoint of the world yet three of them maintained that they were active participants in their religious catholic community. The reason they gave for their involvement was because it provided them with a sense of belonging, as in a kind of club membership, or as part of a 'neo-tribe', as famously put by Michel Maffesoli (1996) as part of the postmodern condition.

Narratives of some participants constantly pointed towards their efforts to negotiate contemporary Western trends with a more conventional orientation of their parents. This was mainly noticeable in the meanings they gave to marriage. Even though most participants saw their future in terms of a career, a great deal of attention was put on their need to get married before their thirtieth birthday. Elena, a rather conventional type of person, told me that she imagined herself married with a family. Elena also saw marriage as a priority before turning thirty, saying that 'otherwise I would be too old'.

With the exception of Mona, most participants constantly stressed that they recognized marriage as an important part of their life course to adulthood and family formation yet at the same time they were willing to postpone it as much as possible.

This was not the case for Luisa, who had just got married during the time of the interview. She was at that time studying for her Master's degree in her early twenties. She said that she never had a job in her life. She started a Master's degree with the hope to find a 'stable' job so that 'at least it would be worth all that studying' and be able to contribute financially to living expenses. Luisa told me:

> The problem today is the loans that we have to pay for a long period of time. My mother freaked out when we told her that we are taking a house loan. My mother helped up a lot financially. My husband had started working when we took the loan and we have to stretch out his wage to pay the loan and pay the bills …. My husband supports me financially. We saved up money to furnish our house. Now it is hard if we want to do something at home. I just paid for my Master's degree plus you have to pay for bills [….] My parents sometimes buy us food.

A key factor underpinning Luisa's account was the way how her close family relations were financially cushioning her sense of anxiety as a newly wed.

Participants emphasized the centrality of the community, family-oriented principles and family obligations in their everyday life, as elucidated by Putnam (1995) on the role of a 'community' with a close network of social relations.

Participants spoke about the way their family was often financially cushioning them by funding their postgraduate education, helping them financially to purchase a car or even contributing financially when buying their first property. In a similar manner to Luisa, Jane also reflected on the way her parents were sheltering herself and her brother from the preoccupations of financial debts. Even though most parents cannot afford to fully financially support their children when buying a property, they tend to find ways to ease this financial burden. Jane referred to a typical solution that some parents in Malta are adopting:

> We thought of redesigning again my mother's house cause my brother is an architect and we were planning to reconstruct the house so I will have the upper floor and he will have the lower floor. But that is a future plan.

The culture of homeownership in Malta, compared to rental tendencies, is still moderately strong amongst millennials when they decide to move into independent living. Whereas in many European countries the changing housing dynamics had upended discourses surrounding tenure norms, homeownership in Malta is still highly regarded. Motives for homeownership are often associated with a source of security and identity (Saunders, 1990). It is linked to a set of values and aspirations underpinning notions of becoming 'better' citizens as 'winners' on the housing market (Vassenden, 2014). The inclination for homeownership is not, however, a feature exclusive to Malta but these values are promulgated across many countries especially other southern European countries such as Italy and Portugal (Azevedo, López-Colás and Módenes, 2016).

Particularly in a culture of strong family network, parents in the south often work hard to mask some of youth's financial difficulties and support their every need especially when buying a property. But to say that young people are doing fine is an understatement. Upon entering independent living, millennials are, more often than not, burdened by house loans. Cognizant of this situation, Andre affirmed that 'in the future I will have to take a house loan. My older sister simply works to pay off her debts.' Participants were all very much aware of the burden to have all their adult life conditioned by a bank repayment schedule and thus they felt they needed to secure a job that earned them enough money to put them in an advantageous position of being able to apply for a house loan. This suggests that their financial situation is assimilated with Kamenetz's (2007) exploration and the way she dubbed this generation as a 'generation debt'.

It is a reality that in most European countries, young people are burdened with the responsibility of financing their own education with the consequence of entering into substantial debts before joining the workforce (Kamenetz, 2007). From her everyday encounters with young people, Kamenetz (2007) clearly illustrated the crisis they are living through as a consequence of the current economic and cultural climate. While it is undoubtedly an American-centric research, its message on the consumer aspirations and financial insecurity of young people is too deeply entrenched and pervasive to be limited solely to US capitalism.

When looking at the applicability of this in Malta, it is worth addressing Malta's social wage, comprising of universal benefits like free healthcare and free education. Unlike the situation of Kamenetz (2007) in America, none of my research participants had taken up loans to finance their first degree mainly because all local undergraduate students at the University of Malta do not pay fees.

In spite of this financial cushioning, young people in Malta are still amongst those who leave their parental home at a later age in Europe. Tying with what was discussed in a previous chapter on prolonging parental dependence, young adult's discourses and imaginaries on the reasons for this prolonging parental dependence, not necessarily tied to financial issues, warrants an examination. The motives for this in Malta are threefold: financial, cultural and geographical.

First, even though Maltese students do not have to pay for their undergraduate studies, they are still not financially independent and rely mainly on their parents' support. The increased years spent in full-time education is delaying their transition of having a full-time job and the possibility to afford independent living.

Second, Malta's relatively high institutionalization of marriage plays a crucial role in youth's decision on when to leave their parental home. All participants, except the newly wed Luisa, were still living with their parents during the time of interview. This was not solely a financial decision for them, but a cultural one. Most participants felt obliged to respect their parents' values and leave home upon marriage. Two respondents said that their parents would not be too pleased if they decided to live on their own before getting married. Elena said that her mother warned her that she would not accept her back home if she decided to leave: 'my mother ... she always says that once we leave, she won't accept us back home, as a tactic to keep her at home until marriage'.

Yet it was not only parental pressure which put them off independent living but, as a general rule, most participants had no interest to live on their own and hoped to remain in partial dependence for as long as possible. They felt free from normative expectations of childhood dependency and in a stage of exploring the variety of possible life directions. They were in a liminal stage, choosing their adult identity by making long-term commitments and decisions. This is in line to Arnett's (2006) definition of 'emerging adults'. Participants admitted that they were living comfortably at their parental home, and enjoyed being financially and emotionally supported. Anthony's reply is a typical reply of their unwillingness to move out:

> I still live with my parents and I will leave when getting married. The reason is that my parents never restricted me in anyway. If I want to go back home at five in the morning, they don't restrict me not to. I don't see why I should leave. Water and electricity bills are sent to my father and I am happy as it is.

Third, it is equally relevant to refer to geographical conditions in Malta. Due to the smallness of the Maltese islands, with an area of 316 km^2, the scope of living on campus while you are a university student does not make much sense. It takes less than an hour, from the other side of the island to reach university and hence students' residences are occupied solely by international students rather than local ones.

Education and the job market

Various studies, as explored in detail in Chapter 2 looked at the way young people in late modernity are lengthening their years in the educational system to be well prepared for the competitive job market. Indisputably, all participants I spoke to put priority on their tertiary education and agreed that they have much more opportunities for post-compulsory education compared to their predecessors.

It is striking to note that their reasons for choosing to pursue higher education was a rather instrumental one – tertiary education was deemed as a tool that guarantees the best 'return value' when going 'job hunting'. Discourse was not surrounded on the real benefits of acquiring new knowledge and equip oneself with cultural capital but it was more interpreted in terms of acquiring the necessary toolkit required for the competitive job market. There was a consensus on their decision to further their education with the hope to better their marketability in the job market by obtaining qualifications needed to find a well-paid full-time employment. Jane said that she felt it was a must to start a second degree right after her undergraduate course, 'right now I'm really anxious. [...] I'm starting another university course because I hate doing nothing. Financially, I want a full-time job to feel more stable.'

This illustrates how choices after compulsory schooling are not done freely but within a climate of increased stress on qualifications. For the majority of these social groups of youth, with opportunities for tertiary education, a university degree has become a universal goal. It is not enough to simply say that youth have greater achievements; they also have greater expectations.

Highly sustained by neoliberal politics, young people are shouldering individual responsibility during times of unemployment, as Bauman (2008) notably puts it, individuals are encouraged 'to devise individual solutions to socially generated problems and to do it individually, using their own skills and individually possessed assets' (Bauman, 2008:4). This is predominantly true for millennials who were trained to believe that one's failure is one's own fault and they take responsibility for personal misfortunes and unanticipated events. With an upsurge on the emphasis placed on credentials in knowledge-based societies, young people are expected to negotiate their way in the labour market as individuals, not as a group. If they fail the system, they are constantly shouldering responsibility for their own performances. In one of my conversations with Sandra, it was clear how strongly she was convinced that unemployment was a matter of personal failure and the individual is to blame for it. She told me, 'I believe that if you really want to work, you will find work.' Typically, this is not just Sandra's perception but a culturally binding mode of attribution – Beck's statement 'your own life – your own failure' is now a mantra. This is one of the implications of neoliberalism. Within this economic context, inequality becomes virtuous – the poor have themselves to blame for their failures. If you are unemployed, it is you to blame for your improvident.

Choices in consumption

Conventionally, it is typical for young people to find temporary jobs, paying pocket-money wages, as well as to put up with jobs they do not want in order to make ends meet during their university years. Some participants spoke about their need to work on part-time basis whilst following a university course. Research published by Eurostudent (2019) reveals that the majority of students (51 per cent) combine studies and paid jobs during the academic year. Most students admit that work has adverse consequences on their academic studies. Reasons for doing so are mainly financial ones, with students often feeling reluctant to work yet they cannot afford not to (Curtis and Williams, 2002).

Coherent to Kamenetz's (2007) observations, most young people I spoke to relied on precarious 'pocket-money' wages from part-time jobs. Andre was very adamant about how dire his financial situation as a full-time student. His biggest expense was running a car – keeping up with maintenance and fuel when relying only on a part-time job as a source of income. He said:

> At the moment I am restricted when it comes to money. Although I have a summer job, the running costs of the car takes most of my money. I spend about 60 euros in fuel and the rest of the money earned is spent during weekends. Then my car broke down and the remaining money which I intended to save was spent on the car.

Owning a car in Malta was highly prioritized by participants as a step towards independence, predominantly due to the penchant of car-dependence in Malta and the somewhat dysfunctional public transport system. With a problem in the density of the car population, Malta is in fact registered as having the third highest number of cars per thousand inhabitants in the EU in 2016 (Eurostat, 2016). Sandra explicitly emphasized the need of having a car as a source for independent mobility. She admitted that although a car is a need rather than simply a want, she found it hard to keep up with its running costs. She told me 'do you think I will survive without my car? And having a car means needing money for fuel.' For Jane owning a car meant becoming self-reliant because 'you don't rely on your parents for transport. I'm looking forward to having my own car so I will be more independent.' Cars were in effect, one of the most-desired consumer products by participants.

Another major expense for participants was technologically mobile devices. The usefulness of technological communication devices such as mobile phones, iPods and laptops stems largely from their portability and accessibility. Participants elaborated on how these devices were essential to provide them with access to information efficiently, with new forms of interfaces that were connecting them to the world. It is increasingly the case that 'the medium, or process, of our time – electric technology – is reshaping and restructuring patterns of social interdependence and every aspect of our personal life' (McLuhan and Fiore (2001 [1967]). Pedagogic training into digital devices for millennials has brought with it a shift in the ways of seeing, talking and behaving in relations to such machines. Andrew Sibley, the Head of Brand and Advertising for Europe for Cisco Networking Systems, in an interview with Brooker (2010) maintained 'to me, a fridge isn't technology. To me, a phone is technology – but it isn't technology to the younger generation that has grown up with it' (Brooker, 2010:554). This distinction in the interpretation of such devices was particularly brought up in the various discussions with participants.

Participants talked me through the increased tendency to buy hire-purchase technological devices with an internet roaming subscription and pay for them on a monthly basis or better still lease them instead. This connects well with what Rifkin (2000) has described when he referred to the shift from ownership to access as part of the everyday reality living in the 'Age of Access'. Such shift makes sense when living in a world where everything becomes quickly outdated with continuous innovation and upgrades which are continuously narrowing product life cycles.

Apart from leasing preferences, schemes to 'buy now and spread the cost with affordable monthly payments' are becoming more attractive yet these schemes play out a weighty burden on the financial situation of youth and in the attitudes towards buying on credit. Debt is assumed as normality and an inevitable part of everyday life for youth.

What was most remarkable was that participants like David felt that he was in 'control' on which brand to choose as an identity marker. Equally in control of his consumer choices, Matthew stressed his desire to have the latest iPhone, as one of the most fetishized devices during the time of the interview: 'I want to buy an iPhone but I don't have the money, probably if I have some money I would buy it'. More than ever brands are regarded as normative mode of identity markers: 'what to wear, what to eat ... all such choices are decisions not only about how to act but who to be' (Giddens, 1991:81). Market researchers, toying with the notion of diversity, are building their brand identities around the different group segments of youth. When speaking to Matthew about fashion, he clearly expressed his ideas of trying to look different instead of following trends. He maintained:

> I try to challenge what others say in order to be different. Sometimes I hate feeling part of the group. When it comes to fashion, I am neither an outcast nor a follower. I don't follow fashion I just buy things I like.

The notion of 'coolness' is constantly shifting itself in an attempt to keep seducing people with its new versions. In using the term 'cool', Matthew meant that 'it is when you break the edge and are no longer mainstream'. In their conquest for 'coolness', millennials are often regarded as being marinated into aggressive advertising that stresses the benefits of consumerism to satisfy artificially created needs (Sklair, 2002, Kamenetz, 2007). Declaring herself as being easily lured by consumer goods, Luisa reflected on her own understanding of consumer seduction. During one of our discussions, she maintained that she couldn't help controlling her spending habits at times, despite declaring that she was always 'financially broke':

> I like spending money, having no control at times. I hate it when I go home without any shopping bags. So thank God that my husband takes care of our money otherwise we would be broke. We recently went to Berlin and I couldn't help not shopping. I had to buy another luggage to come back.

Similar to Luisa, Maria enthusiastically referred to her desires to have branded goods. Yet she admitted that she cannot afford branded goods most of the time because she is financially dependent on her parents. She told me:

I'm not the kind that if my stuff is not branded I won't wear them or use them. I won't search for branded clothes but will love it if I have it. If I find a brand which is bargain, I really like that.

Equally manipulated by aggressive marketing, David saw the 'benefits' in advertisement. He said:

Ads are important because you would be updated on latest products. Like for example when it comes to Apple iphone, there are so many other brands like it but we only know about Apple because it has the name. Adverts create desire I think but it also keeps you updated with latest stuff on the market. I think you need to be updated so you can socialise with others.

On contrary, Mona was very adamant of not being lured by material goods. To the question whether material goods express her identity, she replied:

No, because I don't identify with the things I have. They are material things and for me they mean nothing. So for me the most important thing is that I have the basics, cause there are some things that you need. But consumer goods like branded goods no, I don't need them. Like for example, for coffee at home we are now using fair trade coffee. Things which you can live without we don't buy.

For Mona, environmental activists were the 'cool' ones: 'People who work on things that they believe in. People who are genuine. Things which go beyond trend and there are principles and values involved.' In her critical appraisal of this situation, she commented on the marketing frenzy on consumer goods. Nonetheless, echoing Frank's (1997) observation, resistance to capitalism is being incorporated into the marketing mechanism and simply becoming another market segment of alternative music. Such symbolic contestation is merely taking the form of what it is opposing and becoming absorbed into what McGuigan (2009) called 'cool capitalism'. What is seen as critical of capitalist activity is rapidly absorbed by niche segments and rather than fighting the system, it feeds it.

Although most participants referred to their desire for branded goods, yet the majority of participants were aware of their attitudes not to overspend or enter into unnecessary debts. Most of them proudly declared that they kept their feet firm on the ground and said they never bought something they couldn't afford. David summarized this by saying 'I love Nike. I have to have branded watches ... but ... I am not ready though to buy stuff just to be like others and end up with loans.' Likewise, Jane said that 'I do like them [branded goods] but I buy things that are within my budget. I am practical, I won't buy just because I like it.'

Such characterizations have affinities with the principle to 'save up for a rainy day' as one of the conventional values in Maltese society. Additionally, their financial management training at home also played a crucial role in their spending decisions. Mark, specifically, was trained during childhood to be financially responsible especially when his father passed away and his mother struggled to make ends meet. He declared that he did not have any financial problem:

> I don't really have a problem. My mother ... because of the fact that she brought us up in the absence of my father, always taught us to save money. If I am buying a mobile phone, I won't go for the fancy one but for the cheapest as long as it's functional. I spent some time working part-time and managed to save up some money so if I want to buy a car I won't have to borrow or rely on anyone because I have my own money.

During the focus group, Jane could relate to Mark's way of dealing with his finances. She said she was also trained by her parents to be responsible and not to enter into unnecessary debts:

> My parents always taught us to save money and before I buy something I always ask myself, do I want it or need it? I like saving money. I cannot understand people who do a shopping spree and spend all their money, I wish but I know I can't afford it and also to part with my money, I'm a bit of a Scrooge ... heh I think that during my youth it makes sense to save so I build some solid foundations so if I need money, like for starting my masters, I would have.

Like Sandra who considered herself as quite 'frugal', Jane interpreted her attitudes to money management as being a 'Scrooge' just because she is financially responsible. Sandra believed that her working experience also trained her to be more responsible:

> The fact that I used to work from a young age, although I didn't really need money at sixteen, but I learnt to save money. I admit I am thrifty,

but if I'm on holiday I will spend money. I would prefer to buy a pair of jeans from the market rather than a branded one because it's cheaper.

Compromised choices in the lives of women

The bargaining in choice is evident on different fronts in the life experiences of millennials. However, it is predominately apparent in the lives of young women. The concept of 'compromised choice' is particularly fitting to describe the situation of young female participants. The predisposition for 'compromised choices' is evident in the way they are attempting to strike a balance between their willingness to gratify cultural norms and their desires to design their own life plan.

Changes in expectations and experiences of well-educated young women are becoming more apparent. More women are aspiring to further their studies and have their own career. In the last thirty years, a noticeable shift in the life situation of young women is the increase in educational opportunities resulting in intergenerational social mobility.

Most young females I interviewed during fieldwork were not considering marriage as a goal to be achieved instantaneously. They worked hard to find an intrinsically satisfying activity from which they can earn their own living, without being dependent on a male breadwinner. Jane, typifying a very ambitious self-declared feminist, prioritized having a career instead of starting a family:

> I see myself as a career woman. I don't think so much about having a family. I am more career oriented. Hopefully I would have earned my masters and would be working as a psychologist. People won't look at me as in the shadows of my parents, but for what I am and what I have achieved.

Equally determined to establish herself in her profession as an accountant, Sandra did not see her future in terms of the traditional patriarchal model but sought to construct her life biography. Despite such claims, it is not the case that females in the research location have completely let go of the traditional model of the family. Normative gendered roles still play an important part in the everyday life of youth. Young female participants referred to their need to be independent and have their own career. However, they also imagined their future as married women and mothers.

In their everyday life, with unfavourable structures of family-friendly working conditions, young women face the obstacle of having to combine a career and a family. Most young females planned a career and were very much aware of their future concerns surrounding issues on childcare and career management. They also admitted that they were often encouraged to choose academic courses, like the teaching profession, which offers flexible working hours. It is not a surprise that in Malta the number of females undergoing teaching courses drastically outnumbered that of males. Hochschild (1990) observed similar tendencies amongst female students who were aware of future parental concerns. She maintained that most girls interviewed by Anne Machung

> planned to interrupt their careers from one to five years to have the children but they didn't think this would disadvantage them at work. The students I teach fit this description too. When I show my students a picture of the woman with the flying hair, briefcase in one hand, child in the other, they say she is 'unreal', but they want to be just like her. (Hochschild, 1990:263)

In view of this, it is not accurate to say that young women are completely directors of their own life, choosing their career of their own free-will, divorced from conventional structures. Cultural variables play a crucial role in the way young females with post-compulsory education compromise their choices to satisfy their desires of having a career yet often settle for a family-friendly one that allows them to cope with multiple roles; as an employee, a housewife and a mother.

In spite of the fact that all young female participants had tertiary education and regarded themselves as autonomous to choose their own career paths, Maria and Elena believed that women still have to carry out housework and childcare duties. They maintained that their reaction to such a situation would be to give up their career, for a few years, to stay at home taking care of young children. Elena told me:

> I prefer staying at home and do all the housework myself and take care of the children rather than the man staying at home cleaning the house ....I may

ask him to help out when washing dishes for example. I see with my parents for instance, when my dad tries to help out, my mother always scorns at him that he doesn't do things right. But the question is whether I will be able to afford not working. It's not only finance, the fact that I will be able to bring my own children up is very important for me. I prefer it then taking my children to play school or leaving them with their grandmother.

This apprehension was not felt amongst male participants. They didn't speak about their imaginaries child care concerns. Nonetheless, they still saw the need to have a family later on in life. Anthony asserted that 'I don't imagine myself single all my life. It's because I don't like being alone and it nice to have that significant other in your life.' Showing the need to feel fulfilled and a sense of belonging, Andre declared:

> When I look that far I think I will have my family because it is good to keep the generations going. I see my father enjoying his time with his grandchildren so I would want that. So in the future I would like to have my own family.

Conclusion

While there was broad consensus on the importance to plan out their own life on their own freewill, it was not as straightforward in how it was played out, as Beck and Beck-Gernsheim (2008[2002]), have argued. This chapter drew on various interviews with Maltese millennials in their twenty-something with tertiary education, on their meanings and feelings on their actual life experiences.

This research contributed further to how far the individualization process has advanced, principally when comparing it to the Anglo-American context. Narratives of research participants suggested that it was only in certain roles they felt autonomous. Rather than seen as whole persons, Beck's idea of the fragmented self comes useful here. Young people felt in control when dealing with their future priorities, career choices and travelling options but they did not prioritize, for various reasons, the need to move out imminently from their parental home. At times, their choices were compromised by structural factors as mediated by the family, education and the economic conditions. Such structures continue to have a commanding place in shaping their life course transition into adulthood.

A situation of 'compromised choice' is evident in their partial autonomy. Millennials in the research location are doing informed choices yet still relatively shaped by their family. This degree of compromised choice is displayed in the concessions youth in conservative southern European locations are willing to make to satisfy both cultural norms and their desires to design their own life in line with Western trends.

Summary and conclusions

Speaking about the human condition in the third millennium, Steven Pinker (2018) in *Enlightenment Now* had recently claimed that 'we never had it so good'. According to Pinker, the reasons for this are grounded on the fact that we are now living longer, healthier and have more prosperous lives than ever before, even though we churlishly refuse to accept that we have benefitted from such progress. However, is this really the case?

Without a doubt, Pinker's argument bears some kind of truth. The millennial generation have mastered more control on their lives and have more choices in their personal individualized biography compared to their predecessors. Instead of following a traditional chronological order, millennials within the Anglo-American context are deciding and planning their own life-course transitions.

What became a culturally binding mode of attribution, millennials are regarded as increasingly self-reliant and self-determining agents in how they devise their own life. They are very much aware of the wide diversity of choices in roles in how to live their life compared to their predecessors. They think about their future primarily in terms of personal development, self-branding and as self-entrepreneurs. This generation is also increasingly technologically proficient and live in a world with significant advancement in medicine and health care; as a result, they will probably live longer than previous generations. What's more, millennials also have more opportunities to travel and to use communication devices as their everyday tools.

When it comes to tertiary education, millennials can choose from an array of courses and are more likely to decide to live abroad for the purpose of undertaking tertiary-level studies or work. This process has widespread ramifications especially in contemporary Western societies, with the so-called 'fluid' lifestyles, contextualized within 'knowledge-based' and 'creative' economies. They were born in a climate where, as Giddens puts it, 'no aspects of our activities follow a pre-ordained course, and all are open to contingent happenings' (Giddens, 1991:28).

This book contributes to a trans-disciplinary scholarship on the application of this process of individualization in the lived experiences of well-educated millennials. A number of studies have referred to the concept of individualization (Giddens 1991, Beck and Beck-Gernsheim, 2008[2002], Furlong and Cartmel, 2007[1997]) and the dire situation of living in a neoliberal socio-economic climate (Bauman, 1998, Sennett, 1998, Kamenetz, 2007). However, there are no academic works, to my knowledge, that have made sense of structural and biographical shifts in the life situation of millennials with tertiary education, living in southern Europe, couched in the analysis on individualization and neoliberalism. This book tackled this gap in research.

Through acquiring a sociological imagination, this book promoted a reflexive and critical orientation towards the everyday life of millennials, as a constructed and mutable character rather than as natural and unchanging. The sociological imagination was used to illuminate on the agency of youth through a critical punch on neoliberalism.

The process of individualization itself was treated here as a dialectical process of disintegration and reinvention. Yet it is also a paradoxical one; while it provides for increasing choices for millennials, it nonetheless intensifies anxiety and uncertainty about the future. In a time when 'time-honoured norms are fading and losing their power to determine behaviour' (Beck and Beck-Gernsheim 2008[2002]:7), individuals have more opportunity to live a 'life of one's own' and exercise their own agency in ways that have both benefits and risks. Moreover, millennials are also selecting and organizing their own sequence of life passages not necessarily relying on collective support systems or structures such as the traditional normative structures provided by marriage, gender roles and religious beliefs. As they are now more than ever the directors of their own life, they are also witnessing a threat in predictability and certainty. In the process, contemporary individualized society puts tremendous pressures on individuals and is arguably leaving them dangerously bereft, with no or little sense of communal solace. The growing appetite for excellence, tethering one's own worth to professional achievement, is treated in this book as partly the outcome of the free-market individual.

Notwithstanding the attention put on individual agency, structural constraints such as the shifts in the socio-economic situation are given equal importance in this book. These young adults are not only experiencing greater agency, but the disconsolate part of this period is that millennials are experiencing new forms of regulations within the global neoliberal climate of competition and diminishing job security as well as the increased availability of flexible short-term contract jobs. Within the climate of high rates of youth unemployment, especially in many southern European countries like Greece and Italy, young adults are becoming more apprehensive than ever before and find it natural to spend more time in education. They find it a must to equip themselves with a couple of degrees, knowing that without degrees they do not have very good white-collar employment prospects. Moreover, they are faced with an increasingly flexible job market when they join the workforce. Although short-term job contracts may be sometimes seen as desirable because individuals can diversify their career rather than have a job for life, such a situation often causes anxiety and psychological and financial problems when the contract terminates.

This book framed the understanding of the individualized lived experiences of millennials within the economic shifts from the Keynesian ideology, emphasizing strong government intervention to the economic thinking of Milton Friedman on restricting the role of the market, state spending and support. The heart of neoliberalism, as a kind of 'capitalism unleashed', entails the espousal of coercive competition and the emphasis on market forces over state intervention. Neoliberalism as an ideology was explored in relation to its various predicaments. These include financial meltdown, privatization of public services including health and education, the epidemic of loneliness and a morally corrosive system; all these conditions are blamed squarely on the individual experiencing them.

This book referred to how the neoliberal ideology rests on widespread deregulation of industries and puts effort to solve social and economic problems through market competition and privatization. It is a 'motivated shift away from public-collective values to private-individualistic ones' (Barnett, 2005:7). It explored the conventional wisdom that to prosper within a neoliberal climate, one must risk. Individuals are responsible for their own futures and personal failures specifically during a time when the safety net has gradually dwindled. Millennials are experiencing a decline in the welfare state, cuts in benefits, the selling of state assets, flexibility of working conditions and privatization of health and education. As a result, they habitually live with a taken-for-granted reality of financial burdens and unstable working conditions – a situation that landed themselves the marker 'generation debt'.

Such economic realities were dealt with in this book due to their implications on the 'structure of feeling' of millennials, in other words, the culture of a period with reference to cultural, historical and material conditions which exercise power over behaviour and belief. Millennials' own 'structure of feeling' was examined in terms of 'affective elements of consciousness and relationships' (Williams, 1977:132). To make sense of this 'structure of feeling', this book also unpacked historical and political trajectories influencing lived experiences for youth. Herein, it felt necessary to draw comparisons with other youth generations such as the baby boomers, a generation which experienced economic booming of the post-war years within the Anglo-American context. Baby boomers experienced the expansion and extension of education, which had a direct impact on their advantageous life chances.

What is of substantial interest in this book is how such trajectories within the Anglo-American realities run in the lives of millennials living in southern Europe. How does the peculiar socio-cultural factors, with a relatively strong culture of family networks, clientelism and patronage, present a different reality to millennials in the South?

There are certain characteristics that distinguish southern European countries from the rest of Europe including their religion (mainly Catholicism), strong family relations and their 'delayed' socio-economic processes. Compared to other western locations, the process of individualization, coupled with economic developments and the intensification of neoliberalism, has been 'delayed' in southern locations. Reference was made to various scholars who attempted to define the characteristics of the Mediterranean welfare regimes and outlined the inclination in the South towards family solidarity and dependence, unequal division of family work between the sexes that, in part, restrict participation in the labour force (Guerrero and Naldini, 1997). The institutional particularities of southern European countries, with the predominance of 'familism' (family solidarity and dependency), have substantial impact on employment and family strategies. Primarily, the relatively strong kinship network, the high institutionalization of marriage, the large numbers of inactive women and the prevalence of family-oriented values backed up by religion, explored comprehensively in this book, equally play a major part in inhibiting rather than enabling the spread of neoliberalism in the southern region.

Southern Europe such as Portugal, Spain, Italy, Greece and Malta all have experienced some sort of common socio-economic and political underdevelopment compared to the North due to various factors. What I have called a 'slow-motion development' is partly symptomatic of subjection to authoritarian rule and similar patterns of governance. Mainly due to their colonial status and history of dictatorships, economic developments were not at par with the situation of western Europe. The development of the welfare state, National Health Services and the implementation of subsidized housing, in most countries in the South, happened at a later stage compared to the typical western mode. Moreover, the persistence of socially conservative norms and values limited the spread of neoliberalist practices such as the individualist ethos and the postponement of *laissez-faire* measures.

This book drives home the argument that, although in a 'slower motion' compared to western Europe, individualized lifestyles in a neoliberal economic climate are becoming part of the life situation of youth in the southern European region especially throughout the last twenty years. It is only recently that we are witnessing how neoliberalism is slowly seeping through every crevice of the economic, social and cultural life of individuals. In this regard, the 'slow motion' in the running of an individualized lifestyle suggests how the process of individualization is not a homogenizing process, geared towards producing unified common experiences, but it is considered as having different historical trajectories at different times and places.

This book looked at strategies of negotiation and accommodation, and at times resistance, of cultural conditions with personal agency. It was argued that it is more likely for youth in a southern European research location to balance Western values of modernization with aspects of traditional culture. The situation in the South is not as fluid and free from traditional normative tendencies as in the North. Despite the increasing advancement of the process of individualization, the Catholic Church in southern European countries, as the main supporting pillar in society, is continuously working to promote traditional values. Hence, traditional commitments and support relationships did not lose their significance altogether. Cultural variables are key factors in the way the process of individualization is adopted and adapted.

To explore this further in Chapter 7, I referred to a research I conducted with young people with tertiary education in Malta. This chapter elaborated on the degree of compromised choices demonstrated in the concessions made by youth in southern European locations in their efforts to accommodate and negotiate cultural circumstances including with the network support system typical in the South. Similar to other countries in the South, Maltese society is based on the centrality of family-oriented principles, socially conservative norms and values, intergenerational solidarity and family obligations, and it is deep rooted in communal practices and religious norms. Such cultural particularities are at the heart of what makes young adults' identities and tendencies so distinctive.

Their 'compromised choices' are socially situated and influenced by the synergy between Western individualized influences and the cultural norms of their location at a particular time. This is exemplified in female biographies. Women's liberation from traditional normative gender roles is the major contributing factor in Beck and Beck-Gernsheim (2008[2002]), argument on the development of individualization. In spite of various shifts in females' priorities on how to plan out their lives, young women continuously strive to strike a balance between their desires for a career and their need to satisfy cultural norms. Irrespective of the advancement towards the equalization of the sexes, unlike Becks' assertion of detraditionalization, young women in the southern European locations are not completely released from traditional gender roles; their choices are compromised in line with cultural particularities. This is backed up by European statistics.

Recommendations

This book points to an important area of research in cultural and generational studies which requires further investigation. Research is recommended in the way patterns of employment, including the increasing short-term contracts, coupled with contemporary high rates of unemployment, will continue to have substantial impact on the provision of future pensions for the contemporary youth generation.

A more nuanced exploration of the changes in the life experiences of young people in other locations in southern Europe is needed, to have a better understanding of the complex relationship between structural constraints and individual agency. The framework set out in the last two chapters can be broadened and applied to explore other instances where youth's choices are continuously influenced by other contextual factors and in other locations. It would also be useful to explore the application of individualization to young people with diverse life conditions and chances to assess how the process of individualization transcends to other social groups which may not have opportunities for tertiary education.

Also, further studies are recommended on the intensification of the process of individualization for other generations such as the generation Z, referring to those who came after the millennials and were born at the end of the twentieth century. This generation, currently in their late teens, will be presumably the worst hit with regards to financial problems in the near future. Due to the 'delay' in introducing a neoliberal agenda in post-colonial countries in the South, this generation experienced the affluence of the early 2000s in their childhood. From birth, this generation was fully immersed in the consumerist mentality. Yet they also grew up more aware of global environmental problems compared to previous generations. It would be fascinating to explore how individuals of this generation will experience their young adulthood in what will perhaps be an intensified neoliberal climate. From a very young age, they are voicing their dislike for neoliberal measures and environmental destruction – take the estimated 1.6 million early teens in over 120 countries who left schools on 15 March 2019 to protest climate change and for setting a global movement in the process.

Conclusions from this book are also useful for policymakers for they provide insights on the need for further institutional support for higher education and access of the labour market. Further research in other peripheral locations is also recommended to build on the significance of socio-economic and cultural conditions in the applicability of the process of individualization as a contested process.

End remarks

Sociological notions on imagination imply an understanding of life in the past and in the present and the role of individuals in terms of perception, practice and agency within a given context. Factors underpinning the contemporary life situation of highly educated millennials in southern Europe, both inside and outside academia, are manifold. A consistent dimension in this book is that youth's life situation is both a product of structural socio-economic and political influences as well as the result of subjectivity, choice and agency. By adopting a relational approach, attention was put on establishing in detail the social structures that heavily influence the life experiences of youth. This emphasis might be interpreted as presenting an over-deterministic viewpoint of youth with no room for autonomous decisions. Yet, this book used a holistic understanding of youth by linking culture and social action with wider social structures and material conditions of existence and bridging structure and agency to reflect on the dramatic changes in the life situation of youth.

I conclude with David Harvey's (2005) remarks that 'everything relates to everything else'. Indeed, it bears much truth to say that the concept of individualization cannot be studied divorced from its context. Far from being a homogenous process in the West, it is clearly evident that it has a certain amount of ambivalence. In spite of the fact that youth are more than ever seeking solutions on an individual basis as the Becks have argued, young adults are also deliberately influenced by social structures, specifically by the educational system, the job market and the consumer market. Youth's decisions are not completely autonomous but inclined by what I have called compromised choices. I argued how this process has become well embedded in the life situation of millennials in the South and manifested not only in their working life and everyday decisions but also in their personal conduct.

References

Abela, A.M. (1991), *Transmitting Values in European Malta*, Malta: Jesuit Publications.
Adams, R. (2018), 'Young People Are More Sceptical about the Value of University – Poll', *The Guardian*, 16 August. Available online: https://www.theguardian.com/education/2018/aug/16/young-people-more-sceptical-about-value-of-university-poll (accessed 4 November 2018).
Adorno, T. and Horkheimer, M. (1997), *Dialectic of Enlightenment* (trans.) J. Cumming, London: Verso.
Almog, O. (1998), 'The Problem of Social Type', *A Review, Electronic Journal of Sociology*. Available online: https://www.sociology.org/ejs-archives/vol003.004/almog.html (accessed 5 April 2010).
Alvesson, M. and Skoldberg, K. (2000), *Reflexive Methodology, New Vistas for Qualitative Research*, London: Sage.
Ansprenger, F. (1989), *The Dissolution of the Colonial Empires*, London: Routledge.
Appadurai, A. (1990), 'Disjuncture and Difference in the Global Cultural Economy', *Theory, Culture and Society*, 7: 295–310.
Apple, M. (2004), 'Creating Difference: Neo-Liberalism, Neo-Conservatism and the Politics of Educational Reform', *Educational Policy*, 18: 12–44.
Archer, M. (2000), *Being Human: The Problem of Agency*, Cambridge: Cambridge University Press.
Archer, M. (2003), *Structure, Agency, and the Internal Conversation*, Cambridge: Cambridge University Press.
Argyrou, V. (1996), *Tradition and Modernity in the Mediterranean. The Wedding as Symbolic Struggle*, Cambridge: Cambridge University Press.
Armstrong, G. and Mitchell, J.P. (2011), 'Defence and Attack: Empire, Nation and Resistance in Inter-War Football in Malta', *Social Identities*, 17 (3): 303–320.
Arnett, J.J. (2000), 'Emerging Adulthood: A Theory of Development from the Late Teens through the Twenties', *American Psychologist*, 55 (5): 469–480.
Arnett, J.J. (2004), *Emerging Adulthood: The Winding Road from the Late Teens through the Twenties*, New York: Oxford University Press.
Arnett, J.J. (2006), 'Emerging Adulthood in Europe: A Response to Bynner', *Journal of Youth Studies*, 9: 111–123.
Ashton, D. and Field, D. (1976), *Young Workers*, London: Hutchinson and Co.

Attanasio, O. and Kaufmann, K. (2012), *Education Choices and Returns on the Labour and Marriage Markets: Evidence from Data on Subjective Expectations* (Working Paper), Milan: Bocconi University.

Azevedo, A., López-Colás, J. and Módenes, J.A. (2016), 'Home Ownership in Southern European Countries: Similarities and Differences', *Portuguese Journal of Social Science*, 15 (2): 275–298.

Balogh, T. and Seer, D. (1955), *The Economic Problems of Malta: An Interim Report*, Malta: Government Printing Press.

Barnett, C. (2005), 'The Consolations of "Neoliberalism"', *Geoforum*, 36 (1): 7–12.

Bateman, J. (2018), 'What It Takes to Be Young Greek and Able to Pay Your Bills', BBC Generation Project Online, 13 November. Available online: http://www.bbc.com/capital/story/20181107-what-it-takes-to-be-young-greek-and-able-to-pay-your-bills (accessed 22 March 2019).

Baudrillard, J. (1988), *The Ecstasy of Communication*, New York: Semiotext(e).

Bauman, Z. (1996), 'From Pilgrim to Tourist – Or a Short History of Identity', in S. Hall and P. Du Gay (eds), *Questions of Cultural Identity*, 18–26, London: Sage.

Bauman, Z. (1998), *Globalization – The Human Consequences*, Cambridge: Polity Press.

Bauman, Z. (2000), *Liquid Modernity*, Cambridge: Polity Press.

Bauman, Z. (2007), *Consuming Life*, Cambridge: Polity Press.

Bauman, Z. (2008), 'The Absence of Society', *The Social Evils Series*, New York: Joseph Rowntree Foundation.

Bauman, Z. (2011), *Culture in a Liquid, Modern World*, London: Polity.

Beck, U. (1992), *Risk Society: Towards a New Modernity*, London: Sage.

Beck, U. (1994), 'The Reinvention of Politics: Towards a Theory of Reflexive Modernization', in U. Beck, A. Giddens and S. Lash (eds), *Reflexive Modernization. Politics, Tradition and Aesthetics in the Modern Social Order*, 1–55, Cambridge: Polity.

Beck, U. (1995 [1988]), *Ecological Politics in an Age of Risk* (trans.) A. Weisz, Cambridge: Polity.

Beck, U. and Beck-Gernsheim, E. (1995 [1990]), *The Normal Chaos of Love* (trans.) M. Ritter and J. Wiebel, Cambridge: Polity.

Beck, U. and Beck-Gernsheim, E. (2008 [2002]), *Individualization*, London: Sage.

Beeley, B.W. and Charlton, N.A. (1994), 'Maltese Pattern of Dependence: A Historical Perspective', *Scottish Geographical Magazine*, 110 (2): 112–120.

Bennett, A. (2000), *Popular Music and Youth Culture: Music, Identity and Place*, London: Macmillan.

Bennett, A. (2005), 'In Defence of Neo-Tribes: A Response to Blackman and Hesmondhalgh', *Journal of Youth Studies*, 8 (2): 255–259.

Bennett, T., Savage, M., Silva, E., Warde, A., Gayo-Cal, M. and Wright, D. (2009), *Class, Culture, Class, Distinction*, London: Routledge.

Berger, P.L. and Kellner, H. (1974), 'Marriage and the Construction of Reality', in R.L. Coser (ed), *The Family: Its Structures and Functions*, 157–174, London: Macmillan.

Beveridge, W.H. (1944), *Full Employment in a Free Society*, London: Allen and Unwin.

Black, L. and Pemberton, H. (2004), 'Introduction: The Uses (and Abuses) of Affluence', in L. Black and H. Pemberton (eds), *An Affluent Society? Britain's Post-War 'Golden Age' Revisited*, 1–13, Aldershot: Ashgate Publishing Ltd.

Blackman, S. (2005), 'Youth Subcultural Theory: A Critical Engagement with the Concept, Its Origins and Politics, from the Chicago School to Postmodernism', *Journal of Youth Studies*, 8 (1): 1–20.

Blouet, B. (1993), *The Story of Malta*, Malta: Progress Press Co. Ltd.

Boissevain, J. (1965), *Saints and Fireworks. Religion and Politics in Rural Malta*, London: Athlone Press.

Boissevain, J. (1974), *Friends of Friends: Networks, Manipulators and Coalitions*, New York: St. Martin's Press.

Boissevain, J. (2006), *Hal Kirkop, a Village in Malta*, Valletta: Midsea Books Ltd.

Boltanski, L. and Chiapello, E. (2006), *The Seventh City: The New Spirit of Capitalism*, London: Verso.

Bonke, J. (1995), 'Education, Work and Gender: An International Comparison', IUE Working Paper EUF, 95 (4), Florence: European University Institute.

Borg, C. and Mayo, P. (2008), 'Globalisation, Southern Europe and European Adult Education Policy', *Policy Futures in Education*, 6 (6): 701–717.

Bourdieu, P. (1973), 'Cultural Reproduction and Social Reproduction', in R. Brown (ed), *Knowledge, Education and Cultural Change*, 72–112, London: Travistock.

Bourdieu, P. (1984 [1979]), *Distinction: A Social Critique of the Judgement of Taste* (trans.) R. Nice, London: Routledge.

Bourdieu, P. (1990), 'Structures, Habitus, Practices', in P. Bourdieu (ed), *The Logic of Practice*, 52–79, Stanford, CA: Stanford University Press.

Bourdieu, P. (1998), *Acts of Resistance – Against the New Myths of Our Time*, Cambridge: Polity Press.

Bourdieu, P. and Passeron, J. (1979), *The Inheritors: French Students and Their Relations to Culture*, Chicago: University of Chicago Press.

Bourdieu, P. and Wacquant, L. (1992), *An Invitation to Reflexive Sociology*, Cambridge: Polity Press.

Bowles, S. and Gintis, H. (1976), *Schooling in Capitalist America*, London: Routledge and Kegan Paul.

Brathwaite, J. (2017), 'Neoliberal Education Reform and the Perpetuation of Inequality', *Critical Sociology*, 43 (3): 429–448.

Braudel, F. (1996), *The Mediterranean and the Mediterranean World in the Age of Philip II*, Berkeley: University of California Press.

Briguglio, L. (1995), 'Small Island Developing States and Their Economic Vulnerabilities', *World Development*, 23 (9): 1615–1632.

Brincat, M. (2009), 'The Birth of the "Maltese Model" of Development, 1945–1959', *Journal of Maltese History*, 1 (2): 34–52.

Brooker, W. (2010), 'Now You're Thinking with Portals, Media Training for a Digital World', *International Journal of Cultural Studies*, 13 (6): 553–557.

Buchinsky, M. and Leslie, P. (2010), 'Educational Attainment and the Changing U.S. Wage Structure: Dynamic Implications on Young Individuals' Choices', *Journal of Labour Economics*, 28 (3): 541–594.

Bynner, J. and Côté, J. (2008), 'Changes in the Transition to Adulthood in the UK and Canada: The Role of Structure and Agency in Emerging Adulthood', *Journal of Youth Studies*, 11 (3): 251–268.

Cachia Zammit, A. (1963), 'Malte et l'Migration', *International Migration*, 1 (3): 196–201.

Camilleri, F. (1997), *Women in the Labour Market, a Maltese Perspective*, Msida: Mireva Publications.

Cassar, G. (2009), 'Education and Schooling: From Early Childhood to Old Age', in J. Cutajar and G. Cassar (eds), *Social Transitions in Maltese Society*, 51–74, Msida: Agenda.

Castells, M. (1996), *The Rise of the Network Society. The Information Age: Economy, Society and Culture*, vol. I, Oxford: Blackwell.

Castells, M. (1997), *The Power of Identity. The Information Age: Economy, Society and Culture*, vol. II, Oxford: Blackwell.

Castells, M. (1998), *End of Millennium. The Information Age: Economy, Society and Culture*, vol. III, Oxford: Blackwell.

Chisholm, L. (1995), 'Conclusion: Europe, Europeanisation and Young People: A Triad of Confusing Images', in A. Cavalli and O. Galland (eds), *Youth in Europe*, 127–140, London: Pinter.

Clark, W. (2007), 'Delayed Transitions of Young Adults', *Canadian Social Trends*, 84: 13–21.

Cliquet, R. (2003), *Major Trends Affecting Families*, New York: United Nations.

Cohen, P. (1972), 'Subcultural Conflict and Working Class Community', *Working Papers in Cultural Studies 2*, University of Birmingham, Centre for Contemporary Cultural Studies.

Cohen, S. (1972), *Folk Devils and Moral Panics*, London: McGibbon and Kee.

Coles, R. (1995), *Youth and Social Policy*, London: UCL Press.
Collins, R. (1979), *The Credential Society: An Historical Sociology of Education and Stratification*, New York: Academic Press.
Côté, J.E. (2010), 'The Role of Identity Capital in the Transition to Adulthood: The Individualization Thesis Examined', *Journal of Youth Studies*, 5 (2): 117–134.
Cousins, C. (2000), 'Women and Employment in Southern Europe: The Implications of Recent Policy and Labour Market Directions', *South European Society and Politics*, 5 (1): 97–122.
Crosland, A. (1956), *The Future of Socialism*, London: Jonathan Cape.
Crosland, S. (1982), *Tony Crosland*, London: Jonathan Cape.
Curran, T. and Hill, A.P. (2019), 'Perfectionism Is Increasing over Time: A Meta-Analysis of Birth Cohort Differences from 1989 to 2016', *Psychological Bulletin*, 145 (4): 410–429.
Curtis, S. and Williams, J. (2002), 'The Reluctant Workforce: Undergraduates' Part-Time Employment', *Education and Training*, 44 (1): 5–10.
Debono, M. and Farrugia, C. (2008), 'Perceptions of Globalisation: Attitudes and Responses in the EU – Malta', European Monitoring Centre on Change. Available online: http://www.eurofound.europa.eu/emcc/erm/studies/tn0708016s/mt0708019q.ht (accessed 2 January 2010).
Denzin, N. and Lincoln, Y. (1994), 'Introduction: Entering the Field of Qualitative Research', in N. Denzin, and Y.S. Lincoln (eds), *Handbook of Qualitative Research*, 1–17, California, CA: Sage Publication, Inc.
Denzin, N.K. and Lincoln, Y.S. (eds) (2000), *Handbook of Qualitative Research* (2nd ed.), Thousand Oakes, CA: Sage.
Department of Education (1948), *Report of the Department of Education, 1948/54*, Valletta: Malta.
Department of Education (1960), *Report of the Department of Education*, Valletta: Malta.
Department of Information (1959), *Report of the Department of Education, 1959*, Valletta: Malta.
Di Giulio, P. and Rosina, A. (2007), 'Intergenerational Family Ties and the Diffusion of Cohabitation in Italy', *Demographic Research*, 16: 441–468.
DiMaggio, P. (1987), 'Classification in Art', *American Sociological Review*, 54 (4): 440–455.
Doogan, K. (2009), *New Capitalism? The Transformation of Work*, Cambridge: Polity.
Du Gay, P. (1996), 'Organizing Identity: Entrepreneurial Governance and Public Management', in S. Hall and P. Du Gay (eds), *Questions of Cultural Identity*, 151–169, London: Sage Publications.

Dunford, J. and Sharp P. (1990), *The Education System in England and Wales*, London: Longman.

Dyer, R. (1977), *Stars*, London: British Film Institute.

Easterly, W. and Kraay, A. (2000), 'Small States, Small Problems? Income, Growth, and Volatility in Small States', *World Development*, 28 (11): 2013–2027.

Ehrenreich, B. (2002), *Nickel and Dimed: On (Not) Getting by in America*, New York: Owl Books.

Elder-Vass, D. (2007), 'Reconciling Archer and Bourdieu in an Emergentist Theory of Action', *American Sociological Association*, 25 (4): 325–346.

Elias, N. (2000 [1939]), *The Civilizing Process: Sociogenetic and Psychogenetic Investigations* (trans.) E. Jephcott, Oxford: Basil Blackwell.

Esping-Andersen, G. (1990), *The Three Worlds of Welfare Capitalism*, Cambridge: Polity Press.

European Commission (2011), 'Strategy for Equality between Women and Men 2010–2015', Luxembourg: Publications Office of the European Union.

European Commission (2016), 'Autumn 2016 Economic Forecast: Modest Growth in Challenging Times'. Available online: https://ec.europa.eu/malta/sites/malta/files/ec_autumn_forecast_-_malta.pdf (accessed 20 March 2019).

European Commission (2018), 'Education and Training Monitor'. Available online: https://ec.europa.eu/education/sites/education/files/document-library-docs/volume-2-2018-education-and-training-monitor-country-analysis.pdf (accessed on 10 January 2019).

Eurostat (2009), 'Youth in Europe, a Statistics Portrait', Luxembourg: Publications Office of the European Union.

Eurostat (2016), 'Passenger Cars in Europe'. Available online: https://ec.europa.eu/eurostat/statisticsexplained/index.php/Passenger_cars_in_the_EU (accessed 22 March 2019).

Eurostat (2017), 'Tertiary Education Statistics'. Available online: https://ec.europa.eu/eurostat/statistics-explained/index.php/Tertiary_education_statistics (accessed 30 January 2019).

Eurostat (2018a), 'Young People – Social Inclusion'. Available online: https://ec.europa.eu/eurostat/statistics-explained/index.php/Young_people_-_social_inclusion#Young_people_at_risk_of_poverty_or_social_exclusion (accessed 23 February 2019).

Eurostat (2018b), 'Learning Mobility Statistics'. Available online: https://ec.europa.eu/eurostat/statisticsexplained/index.php/Learning_mobility_statistics (accessed 20 February 2019).

Eurostat, (2018c), 'Bye Bye Parents: When Do Young Europeans Flee the Nest'. Available online: https://ec.europa.eu/eurostat/web/products-eurostat-news/-/EDN-20180515-1 (accessed 20 May 2019).

Eurostat (2019a), 'Government Expenditure on Education'. Available online: https://ec.europa.eu/eurostat/statistics-explained/index.php/Government_expenditure_on_education#Expenditure_on_.27education.27 (accessed 13 May 2019).

Eurostat (2019b), 'Gender Employment Gap in the EU'. Available online: https://ec.europa.eu/eurostat/web/products-eurostat-news/-/EDN-201903071?fbclid=IwAR0Pom092OvYeBmnldpBhHZAB_OH17brWdupV2aT5j7KmehVd53OXnIY8A (accessed 22 April 2019).

Eurostat (2019c), 'Fertility Statistics'. Available online: https://ec.europa.eu/eurostat/statistics-explained/index.php/Fertility_statistics (accessed 22 March 2019).

Eurostat (2019d), 'Euro Area Unemployment at 7.5%'. Available online: https://ec.europa.eu/eurostat/documents/2995521/9935256/3-01072019-AP-EN.pdf/fdd80b34-6c9d-43a2-b2c0-2ce9d4dc3c9c (accessed 10 August 2019).

Eurostat, (2019e), 'Government Expenditure on Social Protection'., Available online: https://ec.europa.eu/eurostat/statisticsexplained/index.php/Government_expenditure_on_social_protection#Expenditure_on_.27social_protection.27 (accessed 13 April 2019).

Eurostudent (2019), 'Motives and Benefits of Working while Studying'. Available online: https://www.eurostudent.eu/download_files/documents/EUROSTUDENT_INTELLIGENCE_BRIEF_52019.pdf (accessed 15 November 2019).

Evans, K. and Furlong, A. (1997), 'Metaphors of Youth Transitions: Niches, Pathways, Trajectories or Navigations', in J. Bynner, L. Chisholm and A. Furlong (eds), *Youth, Citizenship and Social Change in a European Context*, 17–41, Aldershot: Ashgate.

Featherstone, M. (1995), *Undoing Culture: Globalization, Postmodernism and Identity*, London: Sage.

Fenwick, I.G.K. (1976), *The Comprehensive School 1944–1970*, London: Methuen.

Ferguson, M. (1992), 'The Mythology about Globalization', *European Journal of Communication*, 7 (1): 60–93.

Ferragina, E. and Arrigoni, A. (2017), 'The Rise and Fall of Social Capital: Requiem for a Theory', *Political Studies Review*, 15 (3): 355–367.

Ferrera, M. (1996), 'The "Southern Model" of Welfare in Social Europe', *Journal of European Social Policy*, 6 (1): 17–37.

Ferrera, M. (2000), 'Reconstructing the Welfare State in Southern Europe', in S. Kuhnle (ed), *Survival of the European Welfare Systems*, 166–181, London: Routledge.

Ferrera, M. (ed) (2005), *Welfare State Reform in Southern Europe. Fighting Poverty and Social Exclusion in Italy, Spain, Portugal and Greece*, London: Routledge.

Ferrera, M. (2010), 'The South European Countries', in F.G. Castles, S. Leibfried, J. Lewis, H. Obinger and C. Pierson (eds), *The Oxford Handbook of the Welfare State*, 616–629, Oxford University Press, Oxford.

Frank, T. (1997), *The Conquest of Cool: Business Culture, Counterculture, and the Rise of Hip Consumerism*, Chicago: University of Chicago Press.

Freeman, C. (2007), 'The "Reputation" of Neo-Liberalism', *American Ethnologist*, 34: 252–267.

Frendo, H. (1988), *Party Politics in a Fortress Colony: The Maltese Experience*, Valletta: Midsea.

Friedman, M. (1962), *Capitalism and Freedom*, Chicago: University of Chicago Press.

Furlong, A. and Cartmel, F. (2007 [1997]), *Young People and Social Change*, Berkshire: Open University.

Gal, J. (2010), 'Is There an Extended Family Mediterranean Welfare States?', *Journal of European Social Policy*, 20 (4): 283–300.

Galbraith, J.K. (1958), *The Affluent Society*, Boston: Houghton Mifflin Company.

Galea, L. (2003), 'Statistics in Perspective', *The Sunday Times*, 2nd November 2003, p. 15.

Gamble, A. (2001), 'Neo-Liberalism', *Capital & Class*, 25 (3): 127–134.

Geertz, C. (1973), 'Thick Description: Toward an Interpretive Theory of Culture', in C. Geertz (ed), *The Interpretation of Cultures: Selected Essays*, 3–30, New York: Basic Books.

Gergen, K. J. (1991), *The Saturated Self: Dilemmas of Identity in Contemporary Life*, New York: Basic Books.

Gershon, I. (2011), 'Neoliberal Agency', *Current Anthropology*, 52 (4): 537–555.

Gibbs, S. (2019), 'Samsung's $2,000 Galaxy Fold Changes the Smartphone Game', *The Guardian*, 21 February. Available online: https://www.theguardian.com/technology/2019/feb/21/samsungs-2000-galaxy-fold-finally-changes-the-smartphone-game (accessed 21 April 2019).

Giddens, A. (1991), *Modernity and Self-Identity. Self and Society in the Late Modern Age*, Cambridge: Polity.

Gill, R. (2008), 'Culture and Subjectivity in Neoliberal and Postfeminist Times', *Subjectivity*, 25: 432–445.

Giner, S. (1982), 'Political Economy, Legitimation and the State in Southern Europe', *The British Journal of Sociology*, 33 (2): 172–199.

Goldthorpe, J., Lockwood, D., Bechhofer, F. and Platt, J. (1969), *The Affluent Worker in the Class Structure*, Cambridge: Cambridge University Press.

Goodwin, J. and O'Connor, H. (2005), 'Exploring Complex Transitions: Looking Back at the "Golden Age" of From School to Work', *Sociology*, 39 (2): 201–220.

Gorz, A. (1989), *Critique of Economic Reason*, London: Verso.

Gorz, A. (1999), *Reclaiming Work: Beyond the Wage-Based Society*, Cambridge: Polity Press.

Guerra, P. (2018), 'Raw Power: DIY and Underground Cultures as Spaces of Resistance in Contemporary Portugal', *Cultural Sociology*, 12 (3): 241–259.

Guerrero, T. and Naldini, M. (1997), 'Is the South So Different? Italian and Spanish Families in Comparative Perspective', in M. Rhodes (ed), *Southern European Welfare States: Between Crisis and Reform*, 42–66, London: Frank Cass.

Guillén, A. (1996), 'Citizenship and Social Policy in Democratic Spain: The Reformulation of the Francoist Welfare State', *South European Society & Politics*, 1/2 (Autumn): 253–272.

Gutiérrez, R. (2014), 'Welfare Performance in Southern Europe: Employment Crisis and Poverty Risk', *South European Society and Politics*, 19 (3): 371–392.

Hall, S. and Jefferson T. (eds) (2004 [1976]), *Resistance through Rituals: Youth Subcultures in Post-War Britain, Working-Class Youth Culture*, London: Routledge.

Hall, S.G. (1904), *Adolescence; Its Psychology and Its Relations to Physiology, Anthropology, Sociology, Sex, Crime, Religion and Education*, New York: D Appleton and Company.

Halsey, A.H., Heath, A.F. and Ridge, J.M. (1980) *Origins and Destinations*, Oxford: Clarendon Press.

Haraway, D. (1988), 'Situated Knowledges: The Science Question in Feminism and the Privilege of Partial Perspective', *Feminist Studies*, 14 (3): 575–599.

Harding, S. (1986), *The Science Question in Feminism*, New York: Cornell University Press.

Harvey, D. (2005), *A Brief History of Neoliberalism*, Oxford: Oxford University Press.

Hayek, F.A. (1944), *The Road to Serfdom*, London: Routledge and Kegan Paul.

Healey, N. (2008), 'Is Higher Education Is Really "Internationalising"?', *High Education*, 55: 333–355.

Heath, A. (2003), 'Education since 1945', in J. Hollowell (ed), *Britain since 1945*, 296–312, Oxford: Blackwell.

Hebdige, D. (1976), 'The Meaning of Mod', in S. Hall and T. Jefferson (eds), *Resistance through Rituals: Youth Subcultures in Post-War Britain*, 87–96, London: Routledge.

Hebdige, D. (1979), *Subculture: The Meaning of Style*, London: Routledge.

Hebdige, D. (1988), *Hiding in the Light*, New York: Comedia.

Heery, E. and Salmon, J. (eds) (2000), *The Insecure Workforce*, London: Routledge.

Heidegger, M. (1992), *Being and Time*, New York: Harper and Row.

Heinz, W.R. (1991), 'Status Passages, Social Risks and the Life Course: A Conceptual Framework', in W.R. Heinz (ed), *Theoretical Advances in Life Course Research. Volume I Status Passages and the Life Course*, 234–251, Weinheim: Deutscher Studien Verlag.

Herrnstein, R. and Murray C. (1994), *The Bell Curve: Intelligence and Class Structure in American Life*, New York: The Free Press.

Hewitt, P., Flett, G. and Mikail, S. (2017), *Perfectionism: A Relational Approach to Conceptualization, Assessment and Treatment*, New York: Guilford Press.

Hinckle, W. (1967), 'A Social History of the Hippies', in G. Howard (ed), *The Sixties: Art, Politics, and Media of Our Most Explosive Decade*, 207–32, New York: Paragon House.

Hobsbawn, E. (1996), *The Age of Extremes*, New York: Vintage Books.

Hochschild, A. (1990), *The Second Shift*, New York: Avon Books.

Hochschild, A. (1997), *The Time Bind: When Work Becomes Home and Home Becomes Work*, New York: Henry Holt.

Hochschild, A. and Garrett, S. (2011), 'Beyond Tocqueville's Telescope: The Personalized Brand and the Branded Self', *Hedgehog Review*, 13 (3): 82–95.

Hoggart, R. (1958), *The Uses of Literacy*, Harmondsworth: Penguin Books.

Horney, K. (1950), *Neurosis and Human Growth: The Struggle toward Self-Realization*, New York: W. W. Norton.

Howe, N. and Strauss, W. (2000), *Millennials Rising: The Next Great Generation*, New York: Vintage Books.

Hudson, D. (2019), 'Stuff Your Boutique Hotels: The Pissed-Off Residents of Valletta's Capital of Culture', Maltatoday, 24 April. Available online: https://www.maltatoday.com.mt/arts/valletta_2018/94476/boutique_hotels_pissed_off_residents_valletta_capital_culture_malta?fbclid=IwAR3BqcCqruWxxFXy6kUvMxW1n8kwJrFS9aAdZ5-LiwecEucd3UONbECvTuk#.XMlc9WgzZPY (accessed 30 April 2019).

Intergenerational Commission for Resolution Foundation (2019), 'An Intergenerational Audit for the UK: 2019'. Available online: https://www.resolutionfoundation.org/app/uploads/2019/06/Intergenerational-audit-for-the-UK.pdf (accessed 15 June 2019).

International Labour Organization (2017), *Global Employment Trends for Youth 2017 Paths to a Better Working Future* Geneva: International Labour Organisation.

Jenkins, R. (1996), *Social Identity*, London: Routledge.

Johanson, J. and Vahlne, J. (1977), 'The Internationalization Process of the Firm: A Model of Knowledge Development and Increasing Foreign Market Commitments', *Journal of International Business Studies*, 8 (1): 23–32.

Johanson, J. and Wiedersheim-Paul, F. (1975), 'The Internationalization of the Firm: Four Swedish Cases', *Journal of Management Studies*, 12(3): 305–322.

Johnson, P. and Duberley, J. (2003), 'Reflexivity in Management Research', *Journal of Management Studies*, 40 (5): 1279–1303.

Jones, H. (1971), 'The Economic Transformation of Malta in the 1960s', *Scottish Geographical Journal*, 87 (2): 128–141.

Jones, H. (2010), 'Why Students Are Rioting in London', *Time Magazine*, 10 December. Available online: http://content.time.com/time/world/article/0,8599,2036392,00.html (accessed 10 January 2018).

Jones, K. (2005 [2000]), *The Making of Social Policy in Britain from the Poor Law to New Labour*, London: Athlone.

Kamenetz, A. (2007), *Generation Debt*, New York: Riverhead Books.

Kapoor, A. and Coller, X. (2014), 'The Effects of the Crisis: Why Southern Europe?' *American Behavioral Scientist*, 58 (12): 1511–1516.

Karamessini, M. (2008), 'Continuity and Change in the Southern European Social Model', *International Labour Review*, 147: 43–70.

Keightley, E. (2008), 'Engaging with Memory', in M. Pickering (ed), *Research Methods for Cultural Studies*, 175–192, Edinburgh: Edinburgh University Press.

Keightley, E. and Pickering, M. (2006), 'The Modalities of Nostalgia', *Current Sociology*, 54 (6): 919–941.

Kellner, D. (1994), *Media Culture*, New York: Routledge.

King, R. (1979), 'Post-War Migration Pattern and Policies in Malta with Special Reference to Return Migration', *European Demographic Information Bulletin*, 10 (3): 108–128.

Klapp, E.O. (1958), 'Social Types: Process and Structure', *American Sociological Review*, 23: 674–678.

Klein, N. (2005 [2000]), *No Logo*, London: HarperCollins Publishers.

Klein, N. (2007), *The Shock Doctrine: The Rise of Disaster Capitalism*, Toronto: Random House of Canada.

Kohli, M. (1996), *The Problem of Generation: Family, Economy, Politics*, Collegium Budapest: Public Lecture Series.

Kus, B. (2006), 'Neoliberalism, Institutional Change and the Welfare State: The Case of Britain and France', *International Journal of Comparative Sociology*, 47 (6): 488–525.

Lair, D.J., Sullivan, K. and Cheney, G. (2005), 'Marketization and the Recasting of the Professional Self the Rhetoric and Ethics of Personal Branding', *Management Communication Quarterly*, 18 (3): 307–343.

Lasch, C. (1991), *The Culture of Narcissism: American Life in an Age of Diminishing Expectations*, New York: W. W. Norton.

Lash, S. and Urry, J. (1994), *Economies of Sign and Space*, London: Sage.

Latour, B. (1987), *Science in Action: How to Follow Scientists and Engineers through Society*, Cambridge, MA: Harvard University Press.

Lawler, S. (2008), *Identity: Sociological Perspectives*, Cambridge: Polity.

Lawton, D. (2004), *Education and Labour Party Ideologies 1900–2001 and Beyond*, London: Routledge.

Legislative Assembly Debates (23/5/1972), 1st Session, Sitting no. 76, 2260.

Levin, S.T. (2017), 'Millionaire Tells Millennials: If You Want a House, Stop Buying Avocado Toast', *The Guardian*, 15 May. Available online: https://www.theguardian.com/lifeandstyle/2017/may/15/australian-millionaire-millennials-avocado-toast-house (accessed 27 May 2019).

Lieber, R.J. and Weisberg, R.E. (2002), 'Globalization, Culture and Identities in Crisis', *International Journal of Politics, Culture and Society*, 16 (2): 273–296.

Lorenz, C. (2012), 'If You're So Smart, Why Are You under Surveillance? Universities, Neoliberalism, and New Public Management', *Critical Inquiry*, 38 (3): 599–629.

Lupton, D. (1999), *Risk*, London: Routledge.

Maffesoli, M. (1996), *The Time of the Tribes*, London: Sage.

Malta Labour Party Election Manifest (1950), 'Malta First and Foremost, the Labour Party Reaffirms Its Faith', Malta Labour Party. Available online: http://www.maltadata.com/mlp-50.htm (accessed 5 November 2012).

Mannheim, K. (1952), *Essays on Sociology of Knowledge*, London: Routledge Kegan Paul.

Marí-Klose P. and Javier Moreno-Fuentes, F. (2013), 'The Southern European Welfare Model in the Post-Industrial Order', *European Societies*, 15 (4): 475–492.

Marshall, G., Swift, A. and Roberts, S. (1997), *Against the Odds? Social Class and Social Justice in Industrial Societies*, Oxford: Clarendon.

Massumi, B. (2002), *Parables for the Virtual: Movement, Affect, Sensation*, Durham, NC: Duke University Press.

Matthijs, M. (2014), 'Mediterranean Blues: The Crisis in Southern Europe', *Journal of Democracy*, 25 (1): 101–115.

McCrindle, M. and Wolfinger, E. (2010), *The ABC of XYZ, Understanding the Global Generations*, New South Wales: University of New South Wales Press Ltd.

McGuigan, J. (1992), *Cultural Populism*, London: Routledge.

McGuigan, J. (2005), 'Neo-Liberalism, Culture and Policy', *International Journal of Cultural Policy*, 11 (3): 229–241.

McGuigan, J. (2009), *Cool Capitalism*, London: Pluto Press.

McGuigan, J. (2010), *Cultural Analysis*, London: Sage.

McKinnon, R. (2011), 'The Return of Stagflation', *The Wall Street Journal*. Available online: http://online.wsj.com/article/SB10001424052702304066504576341211971664684.html (accessed 8 August 2011).

McLuhan, M. and Fiore, Q. (2001 [1967]), *The Medium Is the Message: An Inventory of Effects*, produced by Agel, J., Corte Madera, CA: Ginko Press.

McRobbie, A. (1994), *Postmodernism and Popular Culture*, New York: Routledge.

McRobbie, A. (2005), 'In the Hood', *The Guardian*, 13 May. Available online: http://www.guardian.co.uk/politics/2005/may/13/fashion.fashionandstyle (accessed 25 October 2007).

Mendras, H. (1997), *L'Europe des Européens: Sociologie de l'Europe occidentale*, Paris, Gallimard.

Mills, M. and Blossfeld, H.P. (2001), 'Globalization and Changes in the Early Life Course', *European Societies or European Society?*, EURESCO conference, Kerkrade, the Netherlands, 6–10 October 2001.

Mintoff, D. (1959), *Malta Demands Independence*, Malta: MLP.

Mitchell, J.P. (2002), *Ambivalent Europeans, Ritual, Memory and the Public Sphere in Malta*, London: Routledge.

Mitchell, W.F. and Muysken, J. (2008), *Full Employment Abandoned: Shifting Sands and Policy Failures*, Aldershot: Edward Elgar.

Moreno, L. (1997), 'The Spanish Development of Southern Welfare', *Working Paper* 97-04/1997. Madrid: Iesa-Csic. Available online: www.Iesam.Cisc.Es (accessed 15 May 2019).

Morgan, S. and Gonzales, L. (2008), 'The Neoliberal American Dream as Daydream. Counter-Hegemonic Perspectives on Welfare Restructuring in the United States', *Critique of Anthropology*, 28 (2): 219–236.

Murray, R. (1988), 'Life after Henry (Ford)', *Marxism Today*, 8–9 October: 11–13.

Myers, M. (2017), *Student Revolt: Voices of the Austerity Generation*, London: Pluto Press.

Nadolny, A. and Ryan, S. (2015), 'McUniversities Revisited: A Comparison of University and McDonald's Casual Employee Experiences in Australia', *Studies in Higher Education*, 40 (1): 142–157.

Nagel, U. and Wallace, C. (1997), 'Participation and Identification in Risk Societies: European Perspectives', in J. Bynner, L. Chisholm and A. Furlong (eds), *Youth, Citizenship and Social Change in a European Context*, 42–55, Aldershot: Avebury.

National Commission for Further and Higher Education (2016), 'Further and Higher Education Statistics 2014–2015'. Available online: https://ncfhe.gov.mt/en/research/Documents/Further%20and%20Higher%20Education%20Statistics/Further%20and%20Higher%20Education%20Statistics%20Report%202014-2015.pdf (accessed 25 October 2017).

National Statistics Office (2018), *Young People on the Labour Market: 2016*, Malta: National Statistics Office.

Newman, K. (1999), *Falling from Grace: Downward Mobility in the Age of Affluence*, California: University of California Press.

Nicolas, J. (1974), 'The Position of Women in the Maltese Economy (1900–1974)', unpublished dissertation, Department of Economics, Royal University of Malta.

Oakley, A. (1981), 'Interviewing Women: A Contradiction in Terms?' in H. Roberts (ed), *Doing Feminist Research*, 30–61, Oxford: Routledge and Kegan Paul.

O'Flynn, G. and Petersen, E.B. (2007), 'The "Good Life" and the "Rich Portfolio": Young Women, Schooling and Neoliberal Subjectification', *British Journal of Sociology of Education*, 28 (4): 459–472.

O'Malley, P. (1996), 'Risk and Responsibility', in A. Barry, T. Osborne and N. Rose (eds), *Foucault and Political Reason: Liberalism, Neo-Liberalism and Rationalities of Government*, 189–208, Chicago: University of Chicago Press.

O'Reilly Mizzi, S. (1994), 'Gossip: A Means of Social Control', in R. Sultana and G. Baldacchino (eds), *Maltese Society: A Sociological Inquiry*, 369–383, Msida: Mireva.

Pakulski, J. and Waters, M. (1996), *The Death of Class*, London: Sage.

Parker, L.D. (2012), 'From Privatised to Hybrid Corporatised Higher Education: A Global Financial Management Discourse', *Financial Accountability & Management*, 28 (3): 247–268.

Penny, L. (2010), 'Smile Till It Hurts', *Soundings*, 45: 136–146.

Pereirinha, J. (1997), 'Welfare States and Anti-Poverty Regimes: The Case of Portugal', in M. Rhodes (ed), *Southern European Welfare States: Between Crisis and Reform*, 198–239, London: Frank Cass.

Peterson, R. and Simkus, A. (1992), 'How Musical Tastes Mark Occupation Status Groups', in M. Lamont and M. Fournier (eds), *Cultivating Differences: Symbolic Boundaries and the Making of Inequality*, Chicago: University of Chicago Press.

Petmesidou, M. and Papatheodorou, C. (eds) (2006), *Poverty and Social Deprivation in the Mediterranean: Trends, Policies and Welfare Prospects in the New Millennium*, London: Zed Books.

Pickering, M. (2008), 'Experience and the Social World', in M. Pickering (ed), *Research Methods for Cultural Studies*, 17–31, Edinburgh: Edinburgh University Press.

Pinker, S. (2018), *Enlightenment Now, the Case for Reason, Science, Humanism, and Progress*, New York: Penguin.

Pirotta, J.M. (1991), *Fortress Colony: The Final Act 1945–1964*, vol. II 1955–1958, Malta: Studia Editions.

Pollacco, C. (2003), *An Outline of the Socio-Economic Development in Post-War Malta*, Msida: Mireva.

Pollock, G. (1997), 'Uncertain Futures: Young People in and out of Employment since 1940', *Work Employment and Society*, 11 (4): 615–638.

Pollock, G. (2002), 'Contingent Identities: Updating the Transitional Discourse', *Young*, 10 (59): 59–72.

Putnam, R.D. (1995), 'Bowling Alone: America's Declining Social Capital', *Journal of Democracy*, 6 (1): 65–78.

Pryce, K. (1979), *Endless Pressure*, Harmondsworth: Penguin.

Quart, A. (2003), *Branded, the Buying and Selling of Teenagers*, New York: Basic Books.

Reay, D. (2009), 'Strangers in Paradise: Working Class Students in Elite Universities', *Sociology*, 43 (6): 1103–1121.

Redhead, S. (1990), *The End of the Century Party: Youth and Pop towards 2000*, Manchester: Manchester University Press.

Reher, D.S. (1998), 'Family Ties in Western Europe: Persistent Contrast', *Population and Development Review*, 24: 203–234.

Rhodes, M. (1997), 'Southern European Welfare States: Identity, Problems and Prospects for Reform', in M. Rhodes (ed), *Southern European Welfare States: Between Crisis and Reform*, 1–22, London: Frank Cass.

Rifkin, J. (2000), *The Age of Access: The New Culture of Hypercapitalism, Where All of Life Is a Paid-For Experience*, New York: Penguin Putnam.

Ritzer, G. (1993), *The McDonaldization of Society: An Investigation into the Changing Character of Contemporary Social Life*, Newbury Park, CA: Pine Forge Press.

Roberts, K. (1996), 'Individualisation and Risk in East and West Europe', in H. Helve and J. Bynner (eds), *Youth and Life Management*, 226–240, Helsinki: Helsinki University Press.

Roberts, Y. (2018), 'Millennials Are Struggling. Is It the Fault of the Baby Boomers?', *The Guardian*, 29 April. Available online: https://www.theguardian.com/society/2018/apr/29/millennials-struggling-is-it-fault-of-baby-boomers-intergenerational-fairness (accessed 10 May 2019).

Robertson, R. (1990), 'Mapping the Global Condition: Globalization as the Central Concept', *Theory, Culture and Society*, 7: 15–30.

Robertson, R. (1995), 'Glocalization: Time-Space and Homogeneity-Heterogeneity', in M. Featherstone, S. Lash and R. Robertson (eds), *Global Modernities*, 25–44, London: Sage.

Rojek, C. (1995), *Decentring Leisure: Rethinking Leisure Theory*, London: Sage.

Romei, V. (2016), 'How Austerity Is Crippling Schools in Southern Europe', *Financial Times*, 11 December. Available online: https://www.ft.com/content/62952f26-be20-11e6-8b45-b8b81dd5d080 (accessed 20 June 2018).

Rose, N. (1999), *Governing the Soul: The Shaping of the Private Self* (2nd ed.), London: Free Association Books.

Rosina, A. and Fraboni, R. (2004), 'Is Marriage Losing Its Centrality in Italy', *Demographic Research*, 11 (6): 149–172.

Rostow, W.W. (1960), *The Stages of Economic Growth: A Non-Communist Manifesto*, Cambridge: Cambridge University Press.

Roussel, L. (1992), 'La Famille en Europe Occidentale: Divergences et Convergences', *Population*, 47 (1): 133–152.

Rudd, P. and Evans, K. (1998), 'Structure and Agency in Youth Transitions: Student Experiences of Vocational Further Education', *Journal of Youth Studies*, 1 (1): 39–62.

Saraceno, C. (1994), 'The Ambivalent Familism of the Italian Welfare State', *Social Politics*, 1 (1): 60–82.

Saunders, P. (1990), *A Nation of Homeowners*, London: Routledge.

Savage, J. (2008), *Teenage: The Creation of Youth 1875–1945*, London: Pimlico.

Schirato, T. and Webb, J. (2003), *Understanding Globalization*, London: Sage.

Schneider, J. (1971), 'Of Vigilance and Virgins: Honour, Shame and Access to Resources in Mediterranean Society', *Ethnology*, 10 (1): 1–24.

Sebastião, J., Capucha, L., Estêvão, P., Calado, A. and Capucha, A. (2013), 'The Asymmetrical Educational Consequences of Economic Recession in Southern Europe'. Available online: https://ecpr.eu/Filestore/PaperProposal/391b74f4-83cd-4ed5-aa37-a8662db55e66.pdf (accessed 23 September 2018).

Sennett, R. (1998), *Corrosion of Character – The Personal Consequences of Work in the New Capitalism*, New York: W. W. Norton.

Sennett, R. (2006), *The Culture of the New Capitalism*, London: Yale University Press.

Simmel, G. (1903 [1997]), 'The Metropolis and Mental Life', in D. Frisby and M. Featherstone (eds), *Simmel on Culture*, 174–186, Sage, London.

Simmel, G. (1950), 'The Stranger', in K.H. Wolff, (ed), *The Sociology of George Simmel*, 402-409, Glencoe: The Free Press.

Sklair, L. (2002), *Globalization: Capitalism and Its Alternatives* (3rd ed.) Oxford: Basil Blackwell.

Social Action Movement (1956), *Memorandum on the Employment of Women and Their Role in Society*, Malta: S.A.M.

Social Mobility Commission (2018), 'Social Mobility Results Poll 2018'. Available online: https://www.gov.uk/government/publications/social-mobility-poll-results-2018 (accessed 3 April 2019).

Stein J. (2013), 'Millennials: The Me Me Me Generation', *Time Magazine*, 20 May. Available online: http://time.com/247/millennials-the-me-me-me-generation/ (12 February 2018).

Sultana, R. (1992), *Education and National Development: Theoretical and Critical Perspectives on Vocational Schooling in Malta*, Msida: Mireva Publications.

Sultana R. and Baldacchino G. (1994), 'Introduction', in R. Sultana and G. Baldacchino (eds), *Maltese Society – A Sociological Inquiry*, 1–21, Msida: Mireva Publications.

Sutton, P. and Payne, A. (1993), 'Lilliput under Threat – The Security Problems of Small Island and Enclave Developing States', *International Studies*, 41 (2): 579–593.

Terdiman, P. (1993), *Present Past: Modernity and the Memory Crisis*, New York: Cornell University Press.

Thornton, S. (1996), *Club Culture: Music, Media & Subcultural Capital*, Connecticut: Wesleyan University Press.

The Times of Malta (1943), 'Expert from Britain Surveys Malta's Educational System, Mr. C. Ellis Reports on His Visit', *The Times of Malta*, 3rd January 1943; page 13.

Toffler, A. (1980), *The Third Wave: The Classic Study of Tomorrow*, New York: Bantam.

Tonkin, E. (1992), *Narrating Our Pasts: The Social Construction of Oral History*, Cambridge: Cambridge University Press.
Trading Economics (2019), 'Malta GDP Economic Rate'. Available online: https://tradingeconomics.com/malta/gdp-growth (accessed 23 June 2019).
Triandafyllidou, A. and Gropas, R. (eds) (2007), *European Immigration: A Sourcebook*, Ashgate, Aldershot.
Tsatsanis, E. (2009), 'The Social Determinants of Ideology: The Case of Neoliberalism in Southern Europe', *Critical Sociology*, 35 (2): 199–223.
Tsekeris, C., Kaberis, N. and Pinguli, M. (2015), 'The Self in Crisis: The Experience of Personal and Social Suffering in Contemporary Greece', Hellenic Observatory, European Institute, 92. Available online: https://www.researchgate.net/publication/316253139_The_Self_in_Crisis_The_Experience_of_Personal_and_Social_Suffering_in_Contemporary_Greece/download (accessed 6 May 2019).
Türken, S., Nafstad, H.E., Blakar, R.M. and Roen, K. (2016), 'Making Sense of Neoliberal Subjectivity: A Discourse Analysis of Media Language on Self Development', *Globalizations*, 13: 32–46.
Uchitelle, L. (2006), *The Disposable American, Layoffs and Their Consequences*, New York: Knopf.
Van Gennep, A. (1960), *The Rites of Passage* (trans.) M. Vizedom and G. Caffree, Chicago: University of Chicago Press.
Vassenden, A. (2014), 'Homeownership and Symbolic Boundaries: Exclusion of Disadvantaged Non-Homeowners in the Homeowner Nation of Norway', *Housing Studies*, 29 (6): 760–780.
Veblen, T. (1999 [1899]), *The Theory of the Leisure Class*, Mineola: Dover.
Viazzo, P.P. (2010), 'Family, Kinship and Welfare Provision in Europe, Past and Present: Commonalities and Divergences', *Continuity and Change*, 25: 137–159.
Vickerstaff, S. (2001), 'Learning for Life? The Post-War Experience of Apprenticeship', Paper presented to the *Work, Employment and Society Conference*, University of Nottingham: 11–13 September 2001.
Vickerstaff, S. (2003), 'Apprenticeship in the "Golden Age." Were Youth Transitions Really Smooth and Unproblematic Back Then?' *Work, Employment and Society*, 17 (2): 269–287.
Visanich, V. (2012), 'Generational Differences and Cultural Change', unpublished PhD diss., University of Loughborough, Loughborough.
Visanich, V. (2015), 'Festa Fandom, Individualised Youth and Cultural Consumption', in A. Azzopardi (ed), *Young People and the Festa in Malta*, 89–108, Best Press: Qrendi.

Visanich, V. (2017), 'Increased Participation in the Festa – A Manifestation of Cultural Omnivores?' in A. Debattista and G. Vella (eds), *Perspectives on Cultural Participation in Malta*, Arts Council Malta, 57–72, Progress Press: B'Kara.

Visanich, V. (2018), 'Autonomy and Anxiety: Changes in the Lived Experiences of Young Women in Malta', *Sage Open*, January – March, 1 – 10.

Walkerdine, V. (2003), 'Reclassifying Upward Mobility: Femininity and the Neo-Liberal Subject', *Gender & Education*, 15 (3): 237–248.

Watkins, S. (2010), 'Shifting Sands', *New Left Review*, 61: 5–27.

Weale, S. (2018), 'Young Adults Most Pessimistic on UK Social Mobility – Poll', *The Guardian*. Available online: https://www.theguardian.com/society/2018/dec/11/young-adults-most-pessimistic-on-uk-social-mobility-poll (accessed 13 May 2019).

Weber, M. (1949 [1904]), 'Objectivity in Social Science and Social Policy', in E.A. Shils and H.A. Finch (eds and trans.), *The Methodology of the Social Sciences*, 50–112, New York: Free Press.

Williams, R. (1965 [1961]), *The Long Revolution*, Harmondsworth, Penguin.

Williams, R. (1977), *Marxism and Literature*, Oxford: Oxford University Press.

Williams, S. (2001), *Emotion and Social Theory*, London: Sage.

Williamson, J. (1978), *Decoding Advertisements: Ideology and Meaning in Advertising*, London: Marion Boyars.

Willis, P. (1977), *Learning to Labour: How Working Class Kids Get Working Class Jobs*, Westmead: Saxon House.

Willis, P. (1978), *Profane Culture*, London: Routledge and K. Paul.

Willis, P. (1990), *Common Culture*, Milton Keyes: Open University Press.

Woods, W. (1946), *Report on the Finances of the Government of Malta*, London: HMSO.

World Bank, Official Website, Gini Index Estimate. Available online: https://data.worldbank.org/indicator/SI.POV.GINI?locations=EU (accessed 12 June 2018).

Wright Mills, C. (1959), *The Sociological Imagination*, New York: Oxford University Press.

Yergin, D. and Stanislaw, J. (1998), *The Commanding Heights – The Battle between Government and the Marketplace That Is Remaking the Modern World*, New York: Simon and Schuster.

Zammit Mangion, J. (1992), *Education in Malta*, Malta: Studia Edition.

Zweig, F. (1963), *The Student in the Age of Anxiety*, New York: Free Press of Glencoe.

Index

abortion 117
academic capitalism 36–8
adbusters 47
adulthood
    emerging 22–3
    financial hardship 33
    reflexive choices 24
    transitional stage 8–9, 14, 16, 20–3
affluence 25, 48, 57, 149
affluent lifestyle 36
Affluent Society, The (Galbraith) 48
Age of Extremes, The (Hobsbawn) 25
agency 4, 7, 24, 43, 46–7, 51–2, 96, 98, 116, 120, 123–4, 144–5
all-inclusive educational system 26–7
Anderson Committee 26
Anglo-American 2, 7, 8–10, 12, 16, 17, 19, 23, 42, 49, 58, 89, 112, 141, 143, 146
Anglo-American context. *See also* Britain
    consumption of production 42
    economic shifts 49
    educational system since 1960s 8–9, 23
    family formation 89–92
    individualization process 112, 141
    life-course transitions 143
    neoliberalism 2, 7
    post-war experience 58–61, 146
    working population 17
anxiety 2, 9, 74, 76, 83, 126–8, 130, 145
Arnett, J. J. 21–3, 125, 132
Ashton, D. 23, 58
Attlee, C. 104
austerity 12–13, 16, 58, 68
austerity measures 13, 35, 58, 68
autonomy 4, 23, 52, 59, 142

baby boomers 15–16, 76–7, 146
Bauman, Z. 5, 21, 23, 73, 94, 124, 133, 144
Beck, U. and Beck-Gernsheim, E. 3–5, 23, 65, 75, 90, 94, 95, 123, 124, 141, 144, 148

Bell Curve (Herrnstein and Murray) 27
Beveridge, W. 26, 60
biographies 3, 14, 23–4
births outside wedlock 91, 99
bohos 46
Boissevain, J. 89, 116
Bourdieu, P. 6, 19, 24, 27, 30–1, 51, 64, 71–2, 122
Bretton Woods agreement 25
Britain 6, 25–7, 32
    educational reforms 19, 26, 30
    hoodie culture 51–2
    intergenerational disparities 77
    National Health Act 79
    tuition costs 35
    university funding cuts 35
    welfare measures 79
British educational reforms 19
Bynner, J. 23, 25, 64, 76, 89, 94

calculability 5, 36
Cartmel, F. 23, 58–9, 120, 144
Catholic Church 86–7, 97, 112, 116
class 1, 15, 26–7, 30–2, 39–40, 46–8, 53, 85
clientelism 10, 92
cohabitation 11, 90–1, 99
Cohen, P. 48
collective conscience 92, 112
Common Culture (Willis) 47
competition 4, 28, 65, 78, 80, 145
compromised choices 10, 120, 139, 142, 148
conspicuous consumption 8, 31, 33, 41–6, 54
consumer seduction 36, 41, 136
consumerism 35–6, 52, 55, 136
    conspicuous structure 43–6
    notion of agency 43–8
    youth seduction 41–2
consumption
    choices 134–9
    cultural 36
    low 28, 66

cool capitalism 45, 137
corporatization 36–7
Corrosion of Character – The Personal Consequences of Work in the New Capitalism (Sennett) 63
Côté, J. 4, 23, 25, 64, 76, 89, 94
counter culture identities 50–4
credentialism 8, 35–6, 54, 127, 133
Crosland, A. 24, 26–7, 79
cultural commonalities 2, 10, 85
cultural impoverishment 48
Cyprus 29, 38–9, 67, 95, 106, 111–12, 115

debt 8, 12, 32, 38, 41, 54, 130–1, 136, 138
Decoding Advertisements (Williamson) 52
decommodification model 87
decommodified welfare 85
destandardization 21
digital mobile devices 82
Disposable American (Uchitell) 65
divorce 90–1, 99, 116

economic growth 5, 25, 58, 61, 79, 101, 111–13
economic security 61, 65, 87
economic underdevelopment 103
Education Act 1944 26
Education and Training Monitor (European Commission Report) 28
educational reforms. *See also* Anglo-American context; Britain; southern European countries
    commodifying public education 27–8
    job market 132–4
    neoliberal strategies 2, 7, 27–8
    social mobility 30–3
entrepreneurial self 80, 83
Esping-Andersen, G. 11, 87–8
ethnic background 15, 19
European Cultural Capital 112
expansion of the educational systems 19–20

fake counterculture 53–4
familialism 2, 11, 85, 94
familism 85, 146
family and kinship networks 11, 85, 91, 115
family obligations 95, 99, 130, 148
family-oriented principles 99, 117, 130, 148

family-oriented values 146
family-owned businesses 103
feeling of apprehension 75
feeling of resentment 73, 76
female participation in the labour market 97–8
Ferrera, M. 11, 67, 86, 88
fertility rates 90–1
Field, D. 23, 58
financial implications
    conspicuous consumption 31, 33, 41–3, 54
    repayment schedule 54–5, 131
    students 35–6
    subcultural activities 36, 43–51, 54
Five Giants 26
flexible capitalism 62
Frank, T. 52–4
Frankfurt school 43
free education 26, 108, 131
free-market economic policy 5–6, 28, 40, 144
'From Pilgrim to Tourist' (Bauman) 21
full employment 21, 25, 41, 57, 128, 133
Full Employment Abandoned (Mitchell and Muysken) 60
Full Employment in a Free Society (Beveridge) 60
Furlong, A. 23, 58–9, 120, 144
Future of Socialism, The (Crosland) 79

gender 19, 27, 53, 68, 85–7, 94–8, 109, 144, 148
gender pay gap 87, 97–8
generation. *See also* millennials
    classification 15–16
    definition 15
    social mobility 19, 33
    university graduates, first 30
Generation X 15
generational differences 16
Giddens, A. 15, 23, 74, 94, 136, 143, 144
Gini index 12
glass-ceiling 87, 97
globalization 16, 37, 40, 43, 64, 72, 80–1
Greece 12, 29, 39, 57–8, 66–8, 77–8, 87, 91, 93, 95, 98, 102, 111–12, 145, 147
Guerra, P. 49
Guerrero, T. 88, 91, 93, 115, 146

Hall, S. 48, 74, 83
Harvey, D. 5–7, 61, 71
Hayek, F. A. 6, 61
higher education. *See also* tertiary education
    in Britain 26–7
    corporatization practices 36–7
    determining factors 27
    grants availability 40–1
    increased access 8
    mass participation 26
    opportunity gaps 19
    southern European countries 29–30, 95, 133, 149
    teenagers 21
hippies 54
hipters 46
Hobsbawn, E. 21, 24, 60, 61
Hochschild, A. 71, 90, 98, 140
Hoggart, R. 48

individualization 1, 6–8, 10–12, 14, 16, 20–2, 24, 26, 28, 64–6, 94, 112, 114–16, 144, 146–50
industrialization 66, 103, 104
inequalities 6, 12, 17, 27–8, 39, 74, 87, 96, 134
institutionalization of marriage 11, 90–1, 99, 131, 146
institutionalized individualism 5
integration proposal 105
intensity of kinship networks 93
intergenerational relations 11, 76, 93, 115
intergenerational solidarity 148
internationalization of students 37
Italy 9, 11–12, 28–9, 38–9, 66–8, 85, 87–8, 90–1, 93, 95, 102, 112, 145, 147

Kamenetz, A. 38, 40, 77, 131, 134, 136, 144
Keynes, J. M. 5–6, 25–7, 59–60, 79, 145
Keynesian organised capitalism 5
Klein, N. 40, 123, 125

labour market
    changes in 1960s 16, 61–5
    educational system, role in 3
    employment regulation 64
    gender inequalities 96–8
    generational polarities 16
    Malta 119, 133, 149

public funds 17
state intervention 25
laissez-faire 6, 112–14, 147
Lampl, P. 32
LEA (Local Education Authority) 27
life course transitions 20–1, 23, 25, 58, 68, 90, 95, 124, 142–3
Long Revolution, The (Williams) 72–3

McCrindle, M. 15, 44
McDonaldization 36–7
McGuigan, J. 31, 45, 49, 72, 82, 112, 137
Macmillan, H. 61
McRobbie, A. 51
McUniversities 36–7
Maffesoli, M. 50, 129
Malta
    agency, notion of 123–6
    colonial and postcolonial status 104–7
    cultural conditions 129–32
    demography, tertiary educated millennials 10, 12, 19
    economic shifts 110–12
    festa-goers 32
    Framework for the Education Strategy for 2014 to 2024 29
    higher education 107–8, 107–9
    industrialization 102–3
    laissez-faire measures 112–14
    private institutions 29–30
    social category or social group 122–3
    socio-economic system 9
    spread of neoliberalism 114–17
    youth unemployment rate 126–8
Mannheim, K. 15
market segments/segmentation 43, 45, 52–3, 67, 137
market-dependency 43, 46
marketing mechanisms 33, 36, 42, 45, 51, 137
marriage 11, 75–6, 89–90, 93, 95, 116, 128–9, 131–2, 139, 144
Marxism and Literature (Williams) 73
Mater Admirabilis Training College 108
'Me Me Me Generation' (Stein) 15
Mediterranean 11, 63, 102, 106
Mediterranean Sea 102
migration patterns 58, 68, 91, 111
millennials. *See also* Malta
    actual lived experiences 7–8

cost of education 2
lived experiences 14–16
negative stereotypes 46
principles of self-interest 78–9
relationship with older generations 76
spending habits 1
tertiary education 1–3
Western societies 2
'Millennials Are Struggling. Is It the Fault of Babyboomers?' (Roberts) 77
mobile technological portable devices 44
mobile workforce 57

Naldini, M. 88, 91, 93, 115, 146
narcissistic personalities 15
neoliberal economy 5, 8
neoliberal policies 79, 91
neoliberal politics 5, 133
neoliberal subjectivity 71, 78–80
neoliberalism. *See also* educational reforms
　Anglo-American context 2
　austerity measures 35
　ideologies 71–8
　individualization 114–17
　labour market 57
　self-fashioning entrepreneurship 71–2
　socio-economic situation 46, 144–50
　South European countries 87–98
　subjectivity 78–84
Nickel and Dimed – on (Not) Getting by in America (Ehrenreich) 63
Normal Chaos of Love (Beck and Beck-Gernsheim) 75
nuclear family 91, 94

omnivorness 32
organized capitalism 69

Pakulski, J. 39
parental home 1, 17, 20, 22, 90, 93–4, 120, 131–2, 141
'patchwork careers' 57
pensions 17, 36, 76–80, 88, 96, 149
perfectionism 9, 80–4
peripheral locations 2–3, 149
personal branding 80–4
Peterson, R. 31
'A Plan for Polytechnics and Other Colleges' 27

Portugal 9, 12, 19, 28–9, 38–9, 49–50, 62, 66–8, 85, 88, 91, 95, 102
postcolonial nation state 107
postcolonial status 104
post-war consensus 25–6
poverty 25, 29, 38–9, 63, 66–7, 75, 79, 85
predictability 36, 74, 127, 144
privatization 2, 6, 27, 107, 114, 145–6

Quart, A. 42

Reay, D. 30
redistribution of resources 79
reflexive modernization 85
religious norms 99, 148
Risk Society (Beck) 74
risks 29, 38–9, 62, 64, 74–5, 79, 86, 112, 126, 144–5
'Robbins Report' 26
Royal University of Malta 108–9

scholarships 38, 108, 144
Second World War 16, 25, 30, 40, 42, 58, 79, 104
secularization 104
self-perfection 82
self-reliance 4–5, 9, 17, 72, 78, 80
semiotics 42, 46, 50, 80
Sennett, R. 62, 63, 71, 74, 144
short-time contracts 17, 39, 57, 62, 64–5, 86, 90, 93, 145, 148
Silent Generation 15
Simkus, A. 31
Simmel, G. 62, 122
slow-motion development 49, 147
snowflakes 15
social exclusion 38–9, 52, 85, 88
social groups. 17, 21, 24, 31, 48, 50, 65, 122, 133, 149
social inclusion 42, 79, 92
social insurance 26, 85
'Social Insurance and Allied Services' (Beveridge) 26
social media 42, 82
social mobility 48, 77, 139
　education and 30–3
　educational system 19–20, 25–6
　omnivore theory 31–2
social networks 3, 74, 91
social wage 25, 79, 131

Social-Darwinism 27
socio-economic changes 2, 8–10, 16, 25, 29, 46, 49, 53, 61, 69, 101–2, 107, 112, 144, 146–7
sociological imagination 3, 13, 144
southern European countries
　early school-leavers 28–9
　economic level 11–12
　educational system, changes in 28–30
　environmental and cultural levels 12
　family and kinship bonds 10–11
　lifestyle mode 12–13, 16
　neoliberal strategies 28
　'slow-motion' cultural changes 49–50, 147
　socio-economic shifts. 8, 10
　teaching quality 29
　welfare arrangements 11
　youth unemployment 66–8
Spain 9, 12, 28–9, 38–9, 57–8, 62, 66–8, 85, 87–8, 91, 95, 102, 111–12, 116, 147
strong kinship ties 11, 14, 89–92
Student in the Age of Anxiety (Zweig) 74
Student Revolt: Voices of the Austerity Generation (Myers) 35
subcultural capital 46–50
subculture 43, 47–51, 54
Sutton Trust charity 32

technological advancement 15–16, 20, 31, 44–5, 61–2, 135, 143
tertiary education
　employment rate 68–9
　job market, Greece 77–8
　in Malta 109, 119–21, 127, 133, 140–1, 143–4, 148–9
　millennials 1–3, 7, 14, 16, 19, 24, 29–33
　public expenditure 38
　social mobile persons 31
　women 95–6
thick description 120
Thornton, S. 50
traditional family 94–5, 98
Tsatsanis, E. 102, 103
tuition fees 13, 32, 35, 38, 40, 54, 109

unemployment
　degree of anxiety 126
　economic challenges 110–13
　Greece's current job market 77–8
　individual responsibility 133
　labour market changes 57–61, 64–5, 93–4
　social security proposal 60
　southern Europe 28–30, 66–9, 86, 145
　state intervention 6
　subcultures of 1970s 49
　youth demography 57
unequal division of family work 146
universities 27, 30, 35–8, 95
　debt generation 38–40
　globalization of 37–8
Uses of Literacy, The (Hoggart) 48

Valletta 112
Veblen, T. 31
Vickerstaff, S. 59

Waters, M. 39
welfare 27, 76, 79, 85–8, 99, 102
welfare state 9, 11, 28, 72, 78–9, 86–8, 96, 102, 107, 145, 147
Western societies 2, 27, 64, 79, 94–5, 143
Williams, J. 134
Williams, R. 72, 73, 146
Williams, S. 41
Willis, P. 19, 27, 43, 48, 49
Wolfinger, E. 15, 44
women
　compromised choices 139–41
　family responsibilities 94–8
　financial independence 97–8
　life choices 139–40
　marriage age 90
　unemployed 57, 68
Wright Mills, C. 3

youth. *See also* millennials
　consumer seduction 41–2
　degree of dependence 93–4
　fake counter-culture 53–4
　individualized lifestyle 71, 74–6
　job market 65
　market dependency 46–50
　risk behaviour 73–4
　subcultures 48–54
youthquake 46

www.ingramcontent.com/pod-product-compliance
Lightning Source LLC
Chambersburg PA
CBHW061836300426
44115CB00013B/2406